THE COMPLETE
ROUGH SHOOT

THE COMPLETE ROUGH SHOOT

John Humphreys

David & Charles

I dedicate this book to the Game Conservancy who
have done so much to improve the quality of our
shooting and our deeper understanding of the
countryside.

Illustrations by Jack Barnard, John Paley
and Dave Parfitt

British Library Cataloguing-in-Publication Data
Humphreys, John
    The complete rough shoot.
    I. Title
    799.2

    ISBN 0-7153-9917-9

Typeset by ABM Typographics Ltd, Hull
and printed in Great Britain by
Redwood Press Ltd,
for David & Charles plc
Brunel House   Newton Abbot   Devon

Contents

Introduction

There are those to whom rough shooting means just what it says, the rough end of the market, a downgrade, poor man's sort of stuff, legalised poaching almost, with the game being shot at close range up the parson's nose, an activity to which no gentleman, far less a lady, would seek to aspire. The adjective is an unfortunate one, I grant you, and I have never been clear whether it refers to the appearance of the sportsmen, the coats of their dogs or the terrain over which they take their sport; 'rough' could at times quite fairly be applied to any or all of them.

However, just as there is nothing coarse about coarse fishing, there is very little rough about the rough shooter. The coarse angler uses line and hooks so fine a trout fisherman would have a job to see them on a dark evening. His tactics, wiliness, adaptability, range of techniques and amount of equipment deemed essential all appear to leave the noble game fisherman nowhere, with his thrashing about, heavy hooks, line like cart rope and apparently

Opposite:
The 4WD vehicle is a useful ally

7

crude approach, especially in the case of the newly spawned reservoir man.

Thus it is with the rough shooter, one unjustly spurned, who for any of a great many reasons has eschewed the formalised ritual of the driven shoot. To him such a sport might smack too much of the artificial and the passive, riddled with the 'after you, Claude' new and old money syndrome which are not for him. He may well not be able to afford such luxury, another reason for seeking a shooting field where he is not charged somewhere not unadjacent to £20 for each pheasant he (or one of his companions) shoots. He sees his shooting as hunting, a key word to which I will return. The rough shooter feels the need to work for his bag, feels that noble birds and beasts of the chase deserve to be worked for, followed into their own territory, outwitted, outlasted, outwalked and in the end fairly killed—although the end result is by no means certain.

A fair illustration was one of many days far away and long ago when I hunted the Bedford Levels accompanied by a self-taught yellow labrador who had picked up his skills 'on the job'. I was armed with a rusty hammergun borrowed from a local farmer—he kept it in his barn to shoot rats and was not really aware that he had loaned it—and on my back a game bag made from the canvas of an old binder; that takes you back a bit. My transport was no fancy jeep or 4WD but an ancient bike which my father had used in his days as an Oxford student.

Once down on the lonely miles of the waterland of the marshes I was free to walk where I chose and as usual set off along the low bank which led to the misty horizon. I was a mile from home and no shot to show for it when old Ajax, my trusty hound (named after a Greek warrior and not the foaming bath cleanser which was launched a month after he was christened), gave a snuffle and a snort, put his head down and began to work what was unquestionably a line.

I followed, thumb on a worn hammer, ready to fire the moment the pheasant showed; such a bird was not to be met with every day and was a prize worth having. We worked that line, old Ajax and I, for two and a half living hours. The trail took us across dykes at which I had to rush and jump, barely landing safely on the far bank, teetering back and clutching at sharp rushes to save me from a wetting, hunting for a plaster to staunch the bleeding. We took unexpected, right-angled turns and followed forgotten droves used years ago by the wash shepherds and haymakers. Sometimes we ground to a halt in an all but impenetrable jungle of reed, thatching rush, sedge and rose-bay willow-herb, the whole knitted into a giant doormat by bell-vine. Surely the bird would have stopped here, but no, the line and the snuffling yellow nose of Ajax took us out of the other side and ever onward.

The pace was leisurely, speeding up a trifle on the shorter grass, but usually a steady walking lope, with time to pause and fill a ruminative pipe, but never allowing the concentration to flag. The chance would come at the most unexpected moment and it was not to be 'fluffed'.

Then at long last, when the bridge where my bike lay carefully hidden was a minor smudge on the skyline, there came the dénouement. The dog paused, hunted round, backtracked and pointed, ears sharp and quizzical, staring intently at the spot *just there* out of my sight, deep in the brown

**The rough shooter seeks out and revels in the
wild places**

stalks. My heart beat, scalp prickled, gun was hefted ready. With a flurry of wings and eruption of colour there sprang a wild, Fenland cock pheasant, wings and tail a flickering blur, jewelled like a Rajah, his choleric chortle of indignation a battle-cry to set the heart racing. Somehow gun found shoulder, hammer snapped back, the shot fired and the bird came clattering down, a pinch of church-window feathers floating on the air. Ajax was there at the fall—well, I said he was no field trialer but he rarely lost a bird due to that shortcoming—and here it was in my hand, truly a moment to be savoured.

The bird was admired, its feathers stroked, loose ones plucked away so that it would look well when I got it home to show my mother. Would I carry it? Far more inconvenient than stuffing it in the bag but it would look so much better when I got it home. I compromised and folded its wings carefully, tucking head beneath one of them and leaving the lovely long tail to poke from the bag flap and not get broken or bent. That was the only shot I had that day and now, forty years later, I recall it in every detail.

9

Last Saturday I shot fifty reared pheasants to my own gun; I do not recall one of them.

Such, then, is what I mean by rough shooting, and my little tale indicates something of what the sport represents to many who follow its magical allure, the hunters who have survived the civilising age, those who work for their sport, who are content with few shots but make each one count. Those who love to work their dogs, sharing canine triumph and disaster as though it were their own, working as a partnership with a spaniel perhaps, half a sandwich each at lunchtime and its ears full of burrs: a dog which hunts, flushes, retrieves, swims like an otter and to which the densest prickles are as a feather bed.

As for the shooter, he must walk far and travel light. No one will carry his equipment for him should he grow weary; no lackeys or keepers attend him, no one brings out his lunch at 1pm precisely. He is a hunter, thrown on his own resources, seeking to outwit his quarry all by himself. When he makes a bag he carries it home and eats what he has shot: no choosing the young and tender, for often such a luxury is denied him. His rule is: if you shoot it, you eat it or make jolly sure that somebody does.

He takes rough weather with smooth, enjoys his own company or that of one or at the most two trusted companions, and keeps his own council. You may find him and his like down on the saltmarshes where the wigeon whistle, curlew weep and wail and the grey geese come. He is out on the freshwater marshes freezing nigh unto death waiting for mallard which fail to come until it is too dark, slogging over a tract of desolate moorland where a pack of grouse is rumoured to live, plodding in the rough grass and nettles alongside the runways of wartime aerodromes, hiding in hedge bottoms waiting for pigeons to see his decoys and come spiralling down from the heavens, or waiting under a cold moon for the geese to swing in to the 'tatty bottom'.

His gear is not fashionable nor fancy; it might raise eyebrows at Six Mile Bottom when the Continental princelings forgather, but it serves him well enough, and is familiar and trusty. Blindfold he could tell his own gun from a hundred similar ones; his boots are old but well greased and sit easy; his old waterproof coat with its capacious pockets contains the modest necessities for his sport.

It is that man and those like him to whom this book is dedicated.

John Humphreys
Bottisham, Cambridge, 1992

1
Going Back a Bit

Predators will be strictly controlled

It was an ancient Chinaman of whom nothing is known who discovered that by mixing sulpur and saltpetre he could make a satisfactory bang. That man has much to answer for: the misery which has resulted from gunpowder-backed propellants will surely not allow him to rest in his urn, although he could hardly be held responsible for the folly of mankind. The fact that he believed he had invented nothing more harmful than a firework would be deemed no defence.

However, without that man there would be no shooting sports and it is equally sure that Man would have devised other means, possibly more vile ones, of dealing death to his brother on a large scale.

The ability to hit a mark at a distance has long been a coveted skill. The legendary feats of the old buffalo hunters and Indian fighters who could shoot their Kentucky rifles with pinpoint accuracy, 'Little' Annie Oakley, the cannoneers of Nelson's navy, the heroes of Fenimore Cooper and the longbow poachers of the medieval woodlands all made it a point of honour to hit that at which they aimed. Before them were the longbowmen who won distinction on battlefields in France, then the crossbow enjoyed a brief reign until the uncertain gunpowder with its inbuilt risk of doing more damage to the firer than the target gradually took over, and in the end ousted all the rest and ruled supreme.

I have at home an old Brown Bess musket. Its original barrel was long and heavy but this was neatly shortened to about thirty inches by a man with a hacksaw and the gun was used for generations as a fowling-piece, spending its final days as a crow-scaring gun. It was doubtless one of many weapons which returned from the wars and left a mysterious gap in the regimental inventory. I would love dearly to have seen piled in one heap the game it had slain during its long history. In our village this weapon was a thing round which rumour and legend accumulated.

'It had,' said an informant who found me a youthful and willing listener, 'a hole halfway up the barrel big enough for a warsp to crawl threw'… 'That was a regular rent day goon; shute a bailiff round a corner afore he'd even seed yer…' Was it this gun or another which was loaded in an emergency with a handful of tintacks when the shot belt was found to be empty? The yarn had it that thus 'stoked up' she was fired at a covey of partridges down on the hard where some rotten boats and heaps of lumber lay. Several birds were seen to be down at the shot, and when the gunner rushed out to retrieve he was alarmed to see half a broken oar rise and be borne slowly and heavily across the river to safety. The tintacks had nailed the birds' wings to the wood, you see. The old gunners in my village were full of 'Gospel truths' like that.

Even further back in history and before the development of the formal driven shoot with its ritual, orchestration and strange rules, all shooting was what is now described as 'rough'. Men in beaver hats walked in sedate line across the weedy stubbles where the hand reapers had left long stalks and where quickset hedges rambled out from overgrown ditches. The fields were small, and the land was a stranger to herbicides and pesticides but was well mucked every autumn in time for the shambling Clydesdales to draw the shining ploughs back and forth each winter like stately ships on the main.

It was a paradise for the old English grey partridge and the coveys would spring with a rusty chirrup at every dozen steps. The long-barrelled flintlocks would be hefted, sparks would fly as lock snapped, squirt of acrid black powder smoke and stab of flame, and a bird would fall fluttering in the thistles. The cry 'Hup!', which was short for 'Muzzles Up', halted the field until the man or men who had fired had gone through the cumbersome process of reloading with the ritual of powder, wadding shot and primer before the line could move again.

To this very day spaniels are trained to sit not with the obvious word of command but still with that old 'Hup!', for the dogs were to drop to shot and wait with the rest until the master was ready again for the fray. Such shooting was a leisurely affair with none of the frenetic rushing onward of sport today. The scene could be transposed easily from low-ground stubble to the high moor where grouse, early in the season, could be walked up in the same way. Look again and the same gentlemen are down on the saltmarsh engaged in what they are pleased to call wildfowling. This

pastime bore little relation to the sport of today with its many restrictions, rules and regulations. In those days and right up to the First World War wildfowling comprised going down to the shore and when you saw a bird—any bird—shooting it.

The flintlocks changed to percussion and still the rough shooter ruled the shooting world. Still the leisurely pace, the laborious reloading, the fustian and frock coats, the paraphernalia of shot flask and ramrod. Still the grey partridge was common and the wild pheasant rare. Still caught up in the Agrarian Revolution, much of the British countryside was ill-farmed, overgrown, poorly drained and a haven for a great variety of species of interest to the sportsman. Few small farmers were concerned about shooting rights, and it was common practice to wander where one wished, only keeping clear of the great estates where the game was strictly preserved.

Sometimes there was trouble. Colonel Peter Hawker took what could best be termed a gang of fellow officers to raid the coverts of his hated enemy Parson Bond, shot many of his reared birds and came away bearing, as well as many pheasants, spoil in the form of a monstrous mantrap which they hung as a trophy upon the mess wall. On another occasion he engaged in a long and acrimonious correspondence with the owner of a local manor about his habit of unauthorised shooting there. The matter was unresolved.

Cambridge University students were no better and ran wild in the remote distances of the undrained and wild fen country near Upware. They shot, among other things, more than enough bitterns, linnets, owls 'and many such little feathered monsters' to constitute an ornithologist's nightmare, but they had free run of countless acres of half-farmed marshland, and in later life graduated to the highest positions in society. Only once did they report encountering opposition: 'Came upon twenty stone of fen farmer standing in a wozzle field; the fat party cutting up rough we decided to beat an orderly retreat'.

Despite such minor setbacks the general picture was one of a rough shooter's paradise with a covey behind every whin, a scattering of grouse on the hills, shore birds, waders aplenty down on the tide and rabbits everywhere. In the eighteenth and nineteenth centuries the sport was certainly one for the well-to-do. The gentry liked to have Mr Gainsborough depict them in full shooting attire accompanied by a leash of shooting dogs which invariably bore a close resemblance to King Charles spaniels. Guns were expensive; it was customary to be attended by a team of men and boys whose task it was to work the dogs, carry the slain, produce the lunch and to work literally as dogsbodies for the gallant sportsmen.

Richard Jefferies said much for the rough shooting countryman in his two great books *The Gamekeeper at Home* and *The Amateur Poacher*. Writing as he did in the days which had just seen the advent of the breech-loader but when the muzzle-loader was still popular, his conclusion was that the rough shooter ought properly to be armed with a matchlock. This weapon was a

chancy bag of tricks, as likely to fail as go off, while the loading and preparing of it to shoot took an age. To hunt with such a piece would remove any taint of greed or accusation of bag-filling on the part of the sportsman and thus ensure that his motives were pure.

The double-barrelled sporting shotgun was designed for use by the rough shooter and even today, when driven shooting is popular and easily available, the old pattern has not changed. The first shot, taken with the front trigger and right-hand barrel of a conventional shotgun, was more open-bored while the second shot came from a barrel with more choke. The object here was clear: the first shot would be taken at a covey rising close

The rough shooter may expect mixed bags

Top:
A bold leap for an over-burdened labrador

Above:
The winning team at the end of the day

Right:
A satisfying sight

18

The sportsman respects the countryside and closes the gates

when open patterns were desirable, and the second, fired when the birds had departed by another twenty yards, required a tighter or more closely choked shot. For driven shooting the reverse would be appropriate, but guns today are still bored on the old pattern developed for walked-up shooting.

The walked-up shooter of the last century would certainly not care to be described as 'rough' in any sense of the word, although such is the name we give to his sport today. It is time we defined our terms. What exactly is rough shooting? It is walking up your birds instead of having them driven towards you; though exceptions will occur when modest, impromptu drives are arranged in miniature by a small group of friends, or the rough shooter might wait for his quarry to come to him, as in duck and goose flighting or pigeon shooting.

The rough shooter will carry his own bag, make his own decisions as to the tactics to employ; will have his own dog, trained by himself, an all-purpose spaniel perhaps, happy to hunt, flush and retrieve, and good in water. He carries his lunch with him and is happiest in his own company or that of one or two friends. He is well versed in the complex legislation affecting his sport, is adept at quarry recognition, and is satisfied with small or non-existent bags. He is no poulterer but is out for the hunt, the walk and just to be in the countryside. He is not fussy about his sartorial elegance but is insistent that his clothing should be practical, warm and dry, with his numerous pockets containing the essentials of his sport and personal needs. Unlike his great-grandfather he will be found only where he has express permission to shoot, for the free old days have gone for good. All that he shoots he will eat or pass on to someone who appreciates it. He might have to be satisfied with a few moorhens, a teal, a crumpled pheasant, a rabbit and a pigeon or two—precious little in fact, but he or his wife will be adept at transforming the most surprising and unprepossessing creatures into tasty meals.

He would not be averse to a day of driven shooting should an invitation come his way and would feel he would be a fool to turn it down, but often he prefers the more natural challenge of the long walks, risks of wettings and snap shots at half-seen birds sprung in the gloaming.

It is a threadbare old saying, but he enjoys being in the open air and doing what comes naturally. Opponents of shooting cannot grasp why it is that a sportsman cannot enjoy the countryside without having to shoot or catch something. It is hard to put the reasons into words, but many a man I know would tramp the highest hills through the most awful weather and midges given the simple incentive of a rod-bag in his hand or a gun on his back. The fact that he may not get a shot or even wet a line matters to him not a jot. He must have something to give purpose to the expedition. His pleasure comes from being part of the natural world in an era of artificiality, of taking a small and sometimes non-existent harvest as did his cavemen ancestors of old.

He is happy to extemporise, unlike the covert shooter who sets off with plans carved in stone, all drives prescribed and the great machinery of beaters, stops, flankers and pegs making a last minute change all but impossible. The rough shooter will sniff the wind, cock his eye at the

western sky and decide to walk *that way* and, a decision made, a path chosen, he sets off across country, his breath puffing out like pipe smoke in the frosty air. He takes any reasonable chance presented to him and turns nothing down, rather like the wet fly man with his reputation for angling for the frying-pan rather than the pure aesthetics of it; good luck to him say I, for that man I know, love and understand.

Those who make an art form of rough shooting use a dog which does not bustle, hunt and flush but is a stately and graceful artist, one which quarters the ground, picks up air scent rather than the foot scent favoured by labrador and springer, quarters in to the squatting bird, makes eye contact and freezes to the spot, bird and dog watching each other, each awaiting the first move. The Hunter/Pointer/Retriever (HPR for short), will wait locked on point until doomsday. The rough shooter can take his time, walk up to the spot, choose his position, kick up the birds and take a measured right and left as the covey springs. That represents 'gentleman's rough shooting'.

There was an old fellow who lived in the next village many years ago; now he is gone to his long home but in his day he was a mighty Nimrod. He rode the High Street on an old bike with a pointer trotting, nose to his back wheel.

Strapped to the crossbar was one of the newfangled Browning automatic shotguns which fired five cartridges as quickly as you could press the trigger. It was not the weapon to turn up with at Sandringham, but such an invitation was unlikely to flip onto the door mat of Arthur's cottage.

He would cycle slowly to the outskirts of the village and cast off the dog into the first stubble field or patch of roots along the way. The nature of the

Opposite:
Choosing your own path—making your own decisions

23

Arthur sorts out the hares, picking a good one

beast is to quarter the ground in great, athletic swathes, that sensitive twitching nose telling it if so much as a mouse is there. On they would go until the dog froze on point. Arthur ground his bike to a halt, leaned it against a post, took out his gun, loaded it from his ragged coat pocket and strolled out towards the dog, taking care to keep downwind of it. He had all the time in the world; the dog would have died of old age rather than move before the word of command.

Arthur paused at the scene of the action, noted which way the birds were lying, rolled himself a thin cigarette, flicked a match, blew out a thin stream of smoke, grunted 'Goo on, then!' and the covey exploded into the autumn sky. The Browning flew up with the speed of light as though of its own volition and five measured shots rang out. It was a matter for surprise when there were not five birds scattered on the stubble when it was all over.

I have made the point that rough shooting does not consist of driving game, but like all generalisations, this one too is wrong. A couple of hunting rough shooters can easily arrange an impromptu drive, whereby one lurks at the end of a quickset hedge and the other taps it down towards him. At another time one might hide behind a drystone wall while his companion makes a great detour and uses the broken ground to flush a gaggle of feeding geese over him—any of a dozen combinations. That's one of the beauties of rough shooting, you see; you may do exactly what you like.

Decoying pigeons or geese is another side of the same coin for it too calls for self-reliance, field-craft, tactics, and standing or falling by your own resources. Bolting rabbits to ferrets was once a grand shotgun sport, a learning-ground for many a country farmer, but since the rabbit plague it has fallen from fashion although some buries lend themselves to it; the all-round rough shooter will find out and exploit such valued spots.

Finally I have included wildfowling in this song of praise to one of the finest shotgun sports. Surely the wildfowler is the epitome of the rough shooter. True, he is an ambusher rather than one who walks up his birds— although even that is not always true—but in terms of finding the wild places, of making his own decisions, of having the chance of precious few shots, he has all the qualifications for a rough shooter's badge. He finds his sport in places where the whiff of danger is never far away; a change in the wind, a sudden fog, a mistaken landmark or a lost compass have all cost coastal gunners their lives.

In the pages that follow my friends and I have tried to present the flavour of the rough shoot and the rough shooter, his dogs, his quarry, his stamping-grounds be they high, low or marshy, his equipment, some advice about shooting straight, (fairly important if you are to have only two shots on one outing), how to be safe, how to shoot pigeons and geese over decoys, and lots more.

The idea is to welcome our reader to our club, for we are not exclusive and suspect that an untried world of new pleasures may await him.

2
What to Shoot

**The little devils will be up to some mischief
once your back is turned!**

It is not so much what, as *where* to shoot which will cause the rough shooter his greatest problems. It is essential that, once he has found his ground, he knows what he is about and shoots only that which it is proper to shoot. As he raises his gun to fire, his brain is making many decisions besides those to do with aiming the weapon and making sure the shot is safe.

He will need to know if the bird is in season or not and whether it is protected. The legitimate quarry species are comparatively few in number and the shooting man or woman must be as sure of them all in their various changes of plumage, ages and sexes as an expert ornithologist. It matters not to a bird-watcher if he makes a mistake, he can always get it right next time, but a shooting man is left gazing ruefully at a dead body with the prospects of appearing in court, losing his shotgun certificate and his permission to shoot that ground, his membership of the BASC and all sorts of reprisals too horrible to contemplate. If he is not sure, he holds his fire.

The shooter owes it to his quarry and his sport to be good at identifying birds, as well as the trees, plants and butterflies he will encounter on his wanderings. He must be able to tell a turtle dove (protected) from a collared

Opposite:
The field boundaries are often more productive than open farmland *(see Chapter 10)*

dove (shootable); a stockdove (protected) from a woodpigeon (shootable); a teal (shootable), from a garganey (protected), and a shelduck (protected) from a mallard. He has no leisurely half-hour to look at brightly coloured plates in a bird book in broad daylight in front of his living-room fire but might have five seconds in poor light with night coming on, his glasses steaming up and snow building up in the west.

On 1 February you may shoot a pheasant (provided it is not a Sunday), but you may not shoot a mallard. You may shoot a mallard in season on a Sunday in Cambridgeshire but not in the old Isle of Ely. You learn this sort of thing because you want to; you have the greatest incentive of all, self-interest. You will study the bird books, take your binoculars, join the local bird club and become an expert, until you can distinguish between the sound of the wing-beats of a shoveler and those of a pochard, the distant gabbling of pink-footed geese from the higher-pitched laughter of whitefronts. When you can do those things you have earned a minor qualification for entry into the shooting field, but not before.

Pheasant

I should be most surprised if there is anyone resident in the UK who does not know a pheasant when they see it. Once a year it appears on a great many Christmas cards. It is by far the most common gamebird and out of every ten quarry species shot in a year in this country, the pheasant accounts for seven of them. The world is full of pheasants with most tropical and temperate countries having an indigenous subspecies; many of these interbreed freely. The pheasants we see strutting by the roadside are mostly cross-bred; almost to a bird they are descended from reared stock put down by shooting estates who seek artificially to boost the number of birds on their ground. It is as well that they do, as without their strays there would be rather less for the rough shooter to hunt.

Who introduced it to this country? The Romans? The Normans? Both have their advocates, but as for me—I could hardly care less as the matter is one of pure speculation and academic interest. More certain is that generations of cross-breeding have given us pheasants which vary from pure white to almost black with the delightful fawn Bohemian phase and the Old English Ringneck thrown in for good measure. The rough shooter will show but passing interest in this information. He might care to know, though, that the dark green melanistic phase is said to be better at holding to his ground and does not stray. I have no proof that such is the case.

The pheasant has been wisely and accurately described as a bird of the borders. It likes the edges of fields, the boundaries of woods, the rough fringes of ditches and hedges and the patches of open ground in the middle of spinneys. The further into a large wood you go the fewer the pheasants. It is a large bird and in the case of the cock very conspicuous but it is a master of disguise, able to hide behind the merest scrap of cover or press itself into a shallow furrow on a bare field and vanish from sight. This is useful information for the rough shooter. He should waste no time struggling through the centres of dense forests but should seek out the clearings and openings and skirt the boundaries. He does not neglect the thinnest cover for he knows that the largest and most dazzlingly beautiful cock pheasant could well be crouching in it.

Like the writer of these lines, a pheasant prefers walking to flying and will run for cover should danger threaten. It will not stop there but will run and run along natural lines of communication from bramble patch to root field, between the rows to the end, sharp right at the dyke and on to the next place, across the road and into the grass verge. Persistence on the part of the shooter and a good dog will eventually run the bird down and only then will it spring aloft with chortle of alarm and blur of wing-beats. In fact it will fly for no more than ten seconds, during which time it will reach astonishing speeds and heights, whereafter it will glide a great distance to the next place of safety where it will pitch and run into cover. It would be surprising were the bird to take wing again that day.

A cock pheasant will have many wives which he protects from rival suitors in the spring. He takes no part in family-raising; this is done entirely by his wives, so it is wise for the rough shooter to take a leaf from the driven shooter's book and go easy on hen pheasants later in the season. The wild hens are the lifeblood of your sport whereas cocks are dispensable. There is a temptation to take a hen on a rough day, especially when no one else is there and you have not had a shot. But to shoot hens late in the year is to eat your own seed corn.

The pheasant lends itself to rough shooting and it can be walked up with dogs provided the shooter sticks to the areas the birds prefer. Hunting dykes, hedges, ditches, small rough fields and spinneys is the favourite and, alone or with a companion or two, the shooter will set off. The pheasant is not an intelligent bird but it is wary and cunning. It will hear you coming at a great distance; it was said that during the First World War the pheasants in Kent crowed when the great guns on the Western Front were firing, sounds inaudible to human ears.

If the rough shooter approaches with great bellowings to his dogs, raucous observations on the weather and instructions to his fellow sportsmen delivered at a volume more suited to the parade-ground than the shooting-field, the pheasants will, not surprisingly, do what they do best and run, not stopping until they have reached a place of safety which might well be off his ground. The rough shooter keeps quiet; he is a hunter and as such blends with the countryside and becomes part of it rather than an intruder in it.

He tries at all times to work into rather than down the wind. For one thing his dog will work far better if the scent of the game is being blown towards him, birds flush more kindly for the walked-up shot if pushed into what wind there is, and game cannot so easily hear the shooter's approach for even the most careful cannot walk in dry bracken without making some sound. The dog will work to the whistle, less frightening to birds than the human voice, and to hand signals, so that the shooter does as little as possible to advertise his approach.

The pheasant will sit tight in cover, invisible to the human eye until the questing nose of the dog pushes it out. Often the dog will indicate that a bird is close and the rough shooter learns to watch it closely. Sudden activity, an over-active tail and sometimes a point (even from springer or labrador) will give due warning of possible action. The shooter prepares to mount, waits that exciting and magical moment when the bird will flush with a blur of wings and explosive burst into the air. In the case of hedges the bird will often have put the cover between him and it and this adds to the excitement, for although almost under his feet the bird might well depart in such a way that a shot is impossible.

My colleagues will be writing about dog work and about how to shoot so I will confine myself to suggesting that you give the bird law. To shoot it the moment it rises is to risk blowing it to smithereens or, more likely, missing it altogether, the pattern of shot having had no time to develop but being still tightly bunched. To shoot would be unsporting and wasteful and betrays an over-anxious beginner more surely than almost anything else. Take your time; let it get away to at least twenty yards before you raise your gun, pick up the line, recall that the bird is surely still rising and that most misses are made underneath and/or behind, and fire your shot.

There is a risk inherent in all rough shooting of wounding, another good reason, if one were needed, for taking a dog. When a bird flies away from the shooter it is concealing its vitals, the head and neck areas, from the pellets and the shot will tend to hit it in the rump. Often all is well but there will be times when a bird will run strongly from what seemed to be a middle-of-the-pattern shot, and in the case of a pheasant falling in thick cover, the shooter is wise to send his dog immediately.

A useful tactic can be employed once you are aware that a pheasant is not a wandering gypsy but has a home territory to which it will head when flushed. If there is a likely wood nearby, or experience has shown you that the birds feeding in this patch have come from *that* direction, then take that into account. Put yourself between the bird and its home and you will be presented with a more testing and efficient shot as it crosses in front prior to heading homewards. You will come to realise the patterns of behaviour of birds on your ground and that is one of the great pleasures, learning your ground, being able to predict with an accuracy which confounds and impresses the stranger exactly which way the bird or the hare will break. This is the beginning of field-craft, one of the great arts.

A refinement of this tactic is to have a dog which works the far side of the cover from the gun. This will have the effect of pushing the bird towards the gun on his own side of the obstruction, rather than giving him the briefest and most tantalising glimpse as it clatters away with the safety of branches in between.

There is another useful dodge which usually presents a more testing target than the straightforward, crude but effective 'shot up the bum'. On the little patch of fen close to my own shoot I see my neighbours weekend after weekend drearily walking their ground, three abreast, back and forth all day in the old rough shooting tradition. They are good shots and effective bag-fillers but they would gain so much more from the experience were they to hide one of their number at the far end of the field, for a great many pheasants rise too far in front to shoot, and fly over the far boundary going like smoke—and fine, testing, opportunist's birds they are.

It requires but two of you to carry out a drive, and one man sent secretly in advance to hide at the end of a hedge or dyke will have many mouth-watering chances denied to the straightforward walker-upper. As well as the pheasant which thought it had beaten the field yet again, he might surprise a magpie slipping down the ash-poles, a rabbit scuttling forward, a pigeon rising early and arrowing past, or even a woodcock flushed from the dry leaves in the dyke bottom. A fox is not an impossibility, but to take advantage of such chances it is essential for the forward gun to approach and take up his position with the utmost stealth and the longest detour which he considers reasonable. If he blows his cover and arrives with too much advance warning, nothing will come his way.

However, the forward gun should do more than simply make his way to his position. By tapping in a flanking hedge or ditch he will move game ahead of him and, with his companion, work an effective pincer movement which pushes game into the miniature drive. If you are mob-handed you may send more than one gun forward and your tactics will increase in complexity the more people you have. It is at such times that knowing your ground and the likely directions of flight are especially useful. With only a few forward guns you do not have the flexibility to make mistakes about over which bush the pheasant is likely to fly.

When driving the game to one or more standing guns it is important that the rules of courtesy common to all shooting fields are observed. The walker should not fire at a bird which is likely to give the forward gun(s) a chance. The object of the drive is not so much to fill the bag but to present a sporting bird. Far better for your friend to have a chance at a well driven pheasant, even if he misses it, than for you to down it after it has managed about four and a half wing-flaps so that the resulting carcass is about good enough for thin soup and little else.

It is possible (although I tend to discourage it) that spectators might wish

to attend your sportings, family, friends or children all anxious to help and see the sport. They can be a mixed blessing for there is not that much for them to do. They become bored if out of sight of the fun and tapping a hedge as a stop all day loses its appeal when the rain falls. They only add to your worries so I advise the rough shooter to leave them at home with his other troubles and travel light.

So much for the pheasant and how to come to terms with it. It is the bread and butter of the lowground shooter and is commonly come by, although once it was so rare that the faintest rumour of one in the parish was enough to rouse the whole population, armed with a battery of crazy weapons, all desperate to bag the bird. In my own boyhood in the Ely Fens it was much the same and a pheasant in the bag was a matter for great rejoicing, for then the partridge was king. Now the roles are reversed.

However, common or not, the pheasant survives only because there are enough people around to feed it in the hard weather, to protect it from its natural enemies when it is nesting and vulnerable, and to plant or encourage a suitable habitat in which it can live. There is a tradition that the rough shooter goes where he wills, shoots what he likes and cares not a damn for the morrow. Ask any keeper what he thinks of those who, making no input themselves, snap around his boundaries and shoot what he considers to be 'his' birds.

To take and give nothing in return has become an expensive luxury. The rough shooter who likes his sport with pheasants has an obligation to do what he can to help. His opportunities and means may be more limited than those of the keepered estate next door, but what is to stop him feeding with a few begged sacks of gleanings when the snow lies thick? Broken bales in the lee of a hedge will save many birds, not only pheasants, from starvation.

Why should he not run a Larsen trap in the spring and thin out the egg-stealing crows and magpies?

No shooting man today can take his sport and give nothing back. There is a new and greater responsibility than once there was, which causes the sportsman to adopt a less predatory guise, to be shown to be a caring user of the countryside, a cropper of a reasonable harvest, not greedy but one who leaves the place at least no worse than he found it. Old-timers might not care for the new way but it is here to stay, like it or not.

The pheasant is safe as long as shooting itself is safe. It is in the interests of the sportsman that there are plenty of birds for him, so he must do what he can to ensure that the feeding, caring and out-of-season work are done. Even the roughest of rough shoots will benefit from the odd head of vermin trapped, sack of corn spread or clump of fir trees planted.

Red Grouse

My old friend Arthur Cadman, that great all-round country sportsman and naturalist, once criticised a shooting book because it chose not to mention the grouse. The author had considered that grouse shooting was so expensive and limited in availability that he would confine himself to easier lowground birds. I see his point but agree also with Arthur, so rather than risk the ire of the great man I include that most prestigious British gamebird in this chapter.

The red grouse is a bird of the high heather moorland and is unique to the UK, being found nowhere else in the world in this particular form. Unlike the pheasant little can be done by mankind to help it. Burning the heather ensures a supply of fresh growth and the control of predators is as useful on the moor as it is on the lowground shoot, while the spreading of grit in places where this essential commodity is scarce is helpful, but by and large the bird is left to itself in the cold and wild places where only shepherds come and go and the curlew weeps and wails.

Subject to wild flunctuations due to cycles of disease, over-populations being followed by sudden dearths, able to survive in many degrees of cold in places where the wind cuts like a razor, but knocked down and killed by a single pellet of number 7 shot, the grouse is an extraordinary bird. It certainly lends itself to both walked-up and driven shooting, and while the purpose of this book is to examine the former, let it be said that as a driven target a pack of red grouse banking round a contour downwind beats all other sporting birds for speed and exciting shooting. No wonder it commands such a high price.

Under-exploited is the grouse as a walked-up bird on remote moors, especially in years when they have bred well. The landowner knows that to leave too great a stock is wasteful; most of the birds will not survive the winter, for any grouse which finds itself without a territory before the hard weather sets in is doomed to be chased from pillar to post until finally it dies of starvation. Far better to shoot the bird heavily and leave a smaller and more effective breeding stock.

Such shooting can cost little and might even be available free from a friendly keeper to someone he knows or who might have helped him as a beater. Often we hear the cry that too many birds are left and where are the guns to shoot them? As the season advances the grouse become wary of being walked up and it is only in deep heather that the wandering gun ought to expect many chances. Early in August when the season opens, traditionally boys' shooting time, the coveys, comprising many birds of the year, sit tight enough and may be walked into quite easily.

Walking up grouse is good sport but can be hard work. The lowground man might be able to rely on a fairly level plain and good going underfoot. When he tires he may stop and take a breather; the distances he has to traverse are not that great. On a heather moor there are peat hags to negotiate, bogs to cross, treacherous green mosses over which to skip gingerly. The hills are steep and grow no more shallow as years pass. A covey chooses to spring about your ears at the very moment when your foot is stuck firmly in a bog, and the other one is groping wildly, seeking a purchase on some slippery cotton-grass, your gun is waving dangerous aloft and your breath heaves in your chest. Try shooting straight with those handicaps and you will know how the walked-up grouse man feels.

However, this is an exciting bird, the cream of the rough shooter's sport, and to hear that harsh cackle or throaty chuckle as a covey rises with a faint whisper of wings, lifting above the bloom of the heather against a backdrop of the finest scenery in these islands, is a rare privilege. Your shots must not be hurried but taken carefully if you are not to be left gazing ruefully after the departing birds with nothing to show for your efforts. The grouse is easy to knock down and retrieve; unlike the pheasant its feathers are loose and thin, which is surprising when you consider the harsh place in which it chooses to live. It is no great runner when down and the treeless landscape in which it is found is a great help when retrieving droppers.

Keep a sharp eye on the departing birds and surprisingly often you will see one peel away and drop out at an amazing distance. Fix your eye on the spot and march resolutely towards it and you or your dog will find the bird there, lying dead. There is a risk in all shooting, especially with wildfowl, grouse and partridges which live in communal groups, of committing the sin of 'browning'. This means firing into the brown or the thick of a pack of rising birds without aiming at a particular one as you should. To 'brown' is considered unsporting and devoid of skill. A purist would not fire at a bird if he felt there was a risk of hitting a second with the same shot.

To aim deliberately at birds packed so thickly that it appears you could hit them with a tennis racquet is not only unsporting but often ineffective. There is more daylight between them than you might imagine and more often than not such a poor shot results in a clean miss or at best a wounded bird—and serve you right! On the other hand, pick a bird carefully and, for some reason which has never been properly explained, another bird or sometimes two or more will fall. If this happens then so be it, but no matter how thick the birds may seem, always pick one to shoot at, stay with it without changing to another which suddenly seems more tempting, and imagine it is the only one in the sky at that second. This is particularly

A 'high bird'

necessary with walked-up and driven grouse, which sometimes appear to cover the sky with their numbers.

The walked-up grouse shooter is far more than a bag-filler and for me he epitomises the ideal rough shooter. If he is one of us effete southerners he travels far for his sport, is content with small bags, earns every shot with blood, sweat, tears and aching legs, carries his own bag, works his dog and is out purely for sport. Best of all he savours some fine countryside, the beauty and grandeur of the heather moor, preserved from choking and encroaching softwood afforestation only by the shooting interest and enlightened landowners. Not only the grouse but whole animal populations and their ecosystems—from frogs to merlins, lizards to harriers, short-eared owls, pipits, wildfowl and golden plover—survive only because of the grouse-shooting interest.

The red grouse fits into the jigsaw, living almost exclusively on heather shoots, preyed upon by peregrine and harrier, its own chicks eating the insects which live in heather, so it plays its part in the delicate balance of the structure. The shooting man too is part of that picture and noted conservationists including the RSPB have acknowledged the part played by

A 'difficult bird'

the moorland shooter and keeper in protecting this increasingly rare and valuable environment.

The rough shooter out after grouse will remain a small minority of our sporting brethren due mainly to the scarcity of the terrain and thus the quarry, but I return to the point that for the man prepared to travel some distance at short notice, take his chance with the local bed and breakfast, walk far and hard and carry his own birds, there is more sport available than he might believe.

I speak of what I know, for I have been lucky enough to shoot grouse on a small moor in North Yorkshire for the last dozen years or so. It is a place of wailing curlew, fluttering pipits and hard slog over some uncompromising country. Take your time and think of it only as putting one foot before the other and it is surprising how far you can travel; mind over matter. There is accommodation in the form of an ancient stone cottage hiding from the gales down in the valley at the foot of the moor, and there is much jollity when, once a year, we assemble there. The size of the bag is low on the list of priorities but it is rare that we come home with nothing and sometimes there might be a couple of brace apiece to take home.

This place of dogs, grey stones, lichen, Swaledale sheep, heather and wet bog-cotton is pure magic, and the possibility of a grouse springing before you at the very next step you take is very much a golden bonus. I end the day totally exhausted, often wet, for when it rains up there it does it with a vengeance, but blissfully at peace, having hunted a wild bird on its own ground and, hit or missed, at least come to terms with it. There might be a snipe, a mallard, teal or a hare in the bag for good measure; but hare-shooting, so far from home and with the dreaded obligation on each of us to carry his own bag, is a matter carefully avoided by the experienced.

This shooting does not cost a fortune and I am far from being a rich man, but my experience shows that even on a modest budget there is grouse shooting to be had if you make enquiries of the right people, contact the sporting agencies or seek information from friends who happen to live in grouse shooting country. Once found, it is a thrilling sport and the pinnacle of a rough shooter's ambition.

Black Grouse, Ptarmigan and Capercaillie

I include these three gamebirds and mention them in passing only for the sake of thoroughness. All are rare, obscure, not the bread and butter of the rough shooter and two of them are subject to surveys set up in reaction to the alarm about their declining numbers.

The black grouse (blackcock and greyhen) is found in the foothills of grouse country, often just below the treeline among the silver birches, or lower down in cotton-grass in hard weather. The blackcock is fair game but as the bird, like the pheasant, is polygamous, it is thought better to spare the hens. The problem is telling the difference between a greyhen and a red grouse which for a moment, as they flush, can look very similar. Errors are often made. A blackcock is a handsome bird to have in the bag and many taxidermists owe their bread and butter to the numerous sportsmen who wish to have their first blackcock stuffed.

The ptarmigan is a subspecies of the red grouse which lives high above the vegetation lines in remote and bleak Scottish mountains. It is very hardy to exist in such wild country and it changes plumage, turning mottled grey, off-white and then snowy white, in order to avoid its enemies in the winter.

To shoot this bird is a thing many wish to say that they have done once, but there is a tendency not to repeat the experiment. To aspire to ptarmigan country calls for mountaineering skills and a degree of fitness which it is not given to all to possess. It might take you half a day to climb high enough into that rocky terrain where gun barrels and ankles are at serious risk from falls and where a sudden hill fog might close in on you and render all your efforts a waste of time.

The ptarmigan have seen so little of mankind, the old enemy, that they are not quite sure how to react but are likely to sit very tight and, when flushed, fly tamely to the next eminence and settle there suicidally, just waiting to be walked up again. Quite often they will fly back past *and below* the shooter so that he finds himself firing down on them as they pass. It might be good to have this experience once to boast you have done it and to keep the taxidermist in further work, but this infrequent gamebird is not a matter for more than passing interest. I prefer to contemplate my ptarmigan from the pages of Archibald Thorburn's plates while seated in my armchair, for he was the artist *par excellence* of this bird.

The capercaillie is the largest gamebird in these islands, the cock weighing in at the fighting weight of an average Christmas turkey, but far less palatable, its flavour having been compared to a blend of whipcord and turpentine—and that by one who sought to flatter. The caper is becoming rare in some of its old haunts; the reasons are debatable and at the time of writing there is a survey afoot by the Game Conservancy to determine the reasons for the decline. There can be little doubt that the dwindling acres of the ancient Caledonian pine forest has much to do with it, as does the increase of foxes and pine martens and a run of poor breeding seasons; but, and this is a personal view, as well as these other factors it has been heavily shot, and considerable inroads into depleted stocks have been made.

The caper is a large and conspicuous bird and an esteemed trophy. Sportsmen from beyond these shores pay great sums to come and shoot one, or preferably more of them. It was tempting for those who had a few caper on their land to capitalise on them in this way. The bird was usually shot driven when it flew with great power and speed, so much so that there were cases of them bursting through steel wire deer-fences.

Found on Deeside, Speyside and Tayside, the caper now remaining are descendants of introduced stock as the bird was once hunted to extinction and its habitat removed during the Industrial Revolution; not really a bird for the rough shooter.

Partridge

There are two species of native partridge shootable in the UK. One is the indigenous English or grey partridge, and the other the French or red-legged partridge and its close relations such as the chukor cross. The two have considerable similarities, but also differences which are significant to the shooting man.

The grey partridge is to many the epitome of the British gamebird, the grouse not excepted: not for nothing has the Game Conservancy adopted it as its symbol. In its heyday it was the commonest lowground sportsman's bird, plentiful in the long stubbles and unkempt hedges where sprays never fell and old-fashioned keepering techniques were practised. The birds rose in endless coveys, sat tight enough for a muzzle-loader to come up to them, could be marked down and walked up a second, third and even a fourth time in the same morning and were delicious to eat.

When driven, the grey partridge would fly in coveys over the hedge behind which the guns were standing. Not as fast as the red grouse, perhaps, the grey is more agile, quicker to react to danger and able to twist on the wing and change its angle of flight and, especially in a wind, burst in a star shell over the guns to provide testing shots, an experience which today is vouchsafed to few shooting men unless they are very fortunate.

In the golden age the East Anglian and Hampshire partridge manors could show sport with wild birds which would produce bags of two or three hundred brace in a day and leave uncountable stocks on the ground.

Sad to say, the grey partridge has fallen on hard times, due almost entirely to modern agricultural practices. The advent of sprays, especially insecticides, took away the vital invertebrate food, notably the sawfly larvae, without which chicks have not a hope of survival. The hedges were grubbed up to create huge fields, 'prairie farming' as it was dubbed, and the sanctuary of the hedge as a nesting site and harbourage for food and shelter also was lost. Where once the bird was plentiful now it teeters on the brink of the chasm of extinction; in Ireland the problem became so acute that all grey partridges are protected, without which measure it is extremely doubtful if there would be any left today.

Better management, the leaving of cereal headlands unsprayed and a renewed planting programme, plus vital research by the Game Conservancy have all helped to arrest the decline, but things do not look good.

As recently as my own boyhood the practice of walking up partridges in September, when the season opened, was common. Back and forth we would tramp across the weedy potato fields which the birds seemed to love for their light soil, lots of weed seeds, shelter and quietness. Every so often a covey would spring aloft with that characteristic rusty chirrup of alarm and we would knock a brace down. By the end of a day it was not unusual to have nine or ten brace weighing heavy in the shoulder-bag. Today that practice would be considered unacceptable. The grey remains a fair mark as a walked-up bird but consistently to shoot them down when their numbers are so low would not be considered responsible or sporting conduct. Another problem—and this applies to all walked-up shooting of gregarious

birds—is that the shooter tends to take the last, closest and slowest to rise and these tend to be the young birds of the year, the very ones he ought to be preserving, while the old stagers which are up and away in a flash are the ones he ought to be shooting.

Having said that, there are still a few treasured places where, when local stocks justify it, walking up partridges over pointers is still carried out and working the birds on sun-drenched, weedy stubbles can be intensely exciting. Like grouse they become more wary and harder to approach as the season advances, but later in the year is a time for driving rather than walking-up. The old dodge was to walk stubbles into roots, for in fields of turnips, mangolds or sugar-beet the birds would sit tight, sometimes too tight, and could be approached easily.

Once I watched a team of well drilled beaters push a huge covey, or more probably the amalgamation of several coveys of greys into a twenty-acre field of short sugar-beet. The beaters drew into the end of this patch and all the standing guns had seen the birds and prepared themselves for a most exciting stand. The beaters came through no more than ten yards apart and not a single bird flushed. The squire was so put out that he commanded the whole field, guns, stops, beaters and spectators to form a line and walk the field back. We did this and then did it again in reverse but not a feather did we flush. They must have lain like stones by our very feet. The grey partridge is a sagacious as well as a charming bird.

It is more usual for the birds to flush well and the problem is to put them

Red-legged partridge, better at running than flying

up within shot. Dogs should not be hunting as for pheasant shooting but ought to be at heel for all grey partridge shooting. As soon as a bird is shot send the dog immediately, for scenting conditions in the dry weather which often coincides with early September are hopeless. As with grouse, a hard-hit bird will fly on and tower; to send your dog for that one might disturb other potential shots so wait until you come close to the spot. The bird is almost always dead so no need to hurry.

Walking-up may be carried out by a team of guns spaced at about thirty-five-yard intervals. Greys have a habit of flying low at first, almost seeming to skim the tops of the leaves. This calls for great care if dogs are out in front or if the covey decides to fly back between the guns; safety is paramount. The more widely spaced the guns are the more likely a covey is to fly low between them.

As with pheasants, small impromptu drives may be arranged by a few people on a rough shooting day. Care must be taken placing the waiting guns as grey partridges are very alert, an old cock in the covey keeping a sharp eye out for intruders and leading the birds away from danger, always departing by a safe route, when trouble threatens. The ease with which the grey can be flushed means that one or two beaters or walking guns can cover quite a large area of stubble (more are needed for thicker cover such as roots), and the forward guns should, if possible, hide behind a hedge, not close to it but a good thirty yards back. The birds will usually leave a field by the same route unless they suspect danger. A rough shooting host who knows his ground will know exactly which are the most favoured flight paths. Walking guns should, it goes without saying, leave singletons and pairs to go forward to the standing guns, although it is acceptable to fire at a covey.

However, I end where I began with a sober caveat to be closely aware of the stocks of grey partridges on your ground. The shooting of them as I have described can be carried on in a very few places where good keeping, sensitive farming and a suitable environment have produced a shootable surplus. A few coveys on your ground justify a few shots and a drive or two at most, but to make heavy inroads is to court disaster. Do not leave it to instinct but carry out proper head-counts, starting in spring when potential breeding pairs, singletons and barren couples may be identified. They are territorial so you should expect to see the same birds in more or less the same place when you go to check.

Breeding success should be carefully monitored. Predators, bad weather and careless agricultural operations all take a toll. The Game Conservancy recommends that if your breeding pairs are averaging two or fewer successfully reared chicks apiece you should suspend shooting altogether. With three or more surviving chicks per pair you ought to be able to take thirty per cent of the stock by shooting, but remember, a run of wet summers and a rogue feral cat are all it takes to turn a moderate success story into disaster.

Those lucky few with regularly shootable stocks of wild grey partridges on their ground are possessed of a pearl of great price, and they husband and cherish it accordingly.

The French or red-legged partridge is superficially similar to the grey but to the sportsman the differences are significant. An introduced species brought here late in the eighteenth century, the red-leg favours the South and East Midlands, not venturing far north of Yorkshire nor west of Dorset. It is more gaudily coloured than the sober grey bird, with white bib, blue and orange flank feathers, black speckled breast, rufous tail and bright red beak and legs.

It lends itself to intensively farmed land and so it is in East Anglia that the bird is often found as a native breeder. However, it is easy to rear and release and has adapted comfortably to the game farm regime. Great numbers of red-legs are released on ground which might be considered unsuitable for them to colonise, so the distribution chart is rather blurred and numerical population assessments are meaningless.

From the sportsman's point of view the main difference between the French and English bird is that the Frenchman will run and the Englishman fly. A pack of greys can be driven more than once during a day but a French partridge will fly over the guns once—often not very well—and that is it for the day. Try to put it up again and it will run and run, either going to thick cover, down a rabbit hole or until caught by a dog. In wet weather it will run until balls of mud accumulate on its feet, becoming in the end great weights the size of golf balls and of a similar density. When it flies it will not take the evasive action of the grey but flies straight and often low over the guns. It is best, therefore, to use any undulating terrain on your ground to show the birds from the top of one ridge and stand the guns at the bottom.

Another difference between the grey and the red-leg is that the red-leg is fond of game-cover strips. It is quite happy creeping about in the bottoms of the kale and sweetcorn patches grown for the pheasants, and when driving such cover, a red-legged partridge is likely to pop out and fly quite well past the guns, giving good shooting. The grey is exclusive to the wide open stubbles and the root fields but the red-leg is not so fussy. A red-leg or two showing with the pheasants provides an interesting challenge to guns who had imagined themselves on terms with pheasants and are then presented with a smaller and slower target.

The prejudice against the red-leg once was such that keepers were instructed to destroy all nests found, partly for the bird's poor sporting qualities and partly because of an erroneous belief that it hindered the breeding of the grey by competing for the same nesting territories. A more legitimate accusation might have been that it mixes freely with the greys and, by its nervous disposition and predilection for running at the least opportunity, it leads the less temperamental greys out of the field as soon as the beaters come into view. As a driven bird it can be disappointing; but to the rough shooter, remember, all is grist to his mill.

There is nothing whatever wrong with a red-leg or a covey of them, springing at your feet with a throaty chuckle from long stubble or field of sugar-beet. That first explosive rush can be exciting and the gun has to be quick to get off his shots before the birds are out of range. The red-leg will appear in unexpected places, sometimes in a thick strip of woodland, from a hedge bottom or the bottom of an overgrown dyke, so it has an added dimension of surprise which puts it quite high on the rough shooter's popularity list. It is common, easily available, a replenishable resource and good to eat, some of the criteria of what constitutes 'a good bird'! Leave the purist sentiments to the driven boys!

On the table red-leg meat is slightly more coarse in texture and flavour than a grey but a young one is, in my view, every bit as tasty. An old red-leg, however, distinguished by knobbly callouses on its legs and by a clear, hard and dark leading edge to the primaries (as opposed to the pale tips of young birds), is useless unless casseroled for a very long time.

The red-leg will sometimes perch on a high place such as a bale stack, barn roof or even in a tree, something a grey will never do.

Duck

Elsewhere in this book appears a list of the duck which are legal quarry species. It behoves the shooting man to be able to distinguish between them all, for ignorance of the law is no excuse for transgressing. As this is not an exhaustive bird book or in-depth wildfowlers' charter, I focus on the salient points of three commonly shot duck and believe that the principles involved apply to other species too. Later in this book John Richards has contributed a chapter on the joys of foreshore wildfowling and there is also a section on inland ponds and the fun to be had with them. However, duck and geese crop up as fair marks for the rough shooter's gun, often in unexpected ways,

**Drake mallard: good in the air, in the bag and
on the plate**

or as the result of the opportunism at which our hero must be adept. A few
basic notes, therefore, might prove in order.

Mallard This bird needs as little introduction as the pheasant for surely
there can be few people who are not familiar with it, if only from feeding
ducks on the park lake. It is a fine sporting bird, a strong flier, great traveller,
wary, exciting and good to eat. It lives in wild and wet places, often marshes
or desolate fens, little highland lochans, damp meadows, salmon rivers and
lonely dew-ponds up on the downlands. It flies out to sea and rests on sandbars, traversing treacherous quicksands and uncrossable creeks, navigating
at night by the stars, here today and in eastern Russia next week. You think I
exaggerate? My friend Dick Mason reared some mallard on his small back
lawn in Leicestershire for the Leicester Wildfowlers' Association of which he
was a member. One of his ringed birds was shot in far eastern Russia two
weeks after being released on an estate lake in Dick's neighbouring village. It
is that romantic element of which all wildfowl are possessed which makes
them special and a different thing from the parochial pheasant which spends
its whole life within four fields of where it was hatched.

Duck tend to feed at night and rest during the day. This means that sport
with them is best at the magic hours of dawn and dusk when the birds fly to
and from feeding and resting grounds. The day they will spend on a sandbar, or some great lake or reservoir, safe from foxes, flying out as night falls

September fowler with a mixed bag

to a place of which only they know, be it an old potato field, a stubble, a patch of laid corn or even your own little flight pond. The rough shooter interested in mallard makes it his business to know such things, and should be able to watch the great flights arrowing over high in the autumn skies, work out where they are headed and make the necessary plans to ambush them.

More often a rough shooter will blunder across small parties during his sorties through the fields. Mallard will often spend their days in a quiet dyke in undisturbed fields or resting on quite a small pond. At the approach of the gun they will spring aloft with quacks of alarm and present good going-away shots. A careful shooter ought to get two each time, but due to excitement, hurrying and over-eagerness they are sometimes missed—behind and below, like most things we miss.

A shot like that and a mallard or two in the bag is a real bonus on a knockabout sort of day and here again, a man who knows his ground will become aware that mallard have one or two favourite places to which they return time after time and where a shot will sometimes be possible. The birds have sharp hearing and a keen sense of smell so you ought to approach such places upwind and keep quiet, with dogs well at heel. Such a practice should not be overdone and the birds stalked in this way no more often than once a fortnight at the most. They will become distrustful of the place and move away, taking with them a valuable asset from your shoot.

46

For morning flight when the birds are leaving their feeding grounds the gunner should be in position to intercept them well before daylight. Even in pitch dark he will hear birds on the move and will distinguish the guttural chattering of the mallard, the thin whistle of wigeon and the different rhythm and sound of their wing-beats. As the sky pales he will see the black blobs on the curtain of the dawn and here again his quarry identification is put to the test with only silhouettes upon which to base his judgements. He should be well hidden in the reeds or behind some camouflage netting, for wildfowl are very sharp-sighted and the movements of a man hidden below them or his white face and hands bobbing about in the gloom will turn them more quickly than anything, and deny him a shot.

A dog is essential for this as for all other forms of rough shooting. A wounded duck planing down in the half-light is virtually unpickable by a human unaided, for the bird will dive and hide on reaching water or will run and squat like a stone in cover if it lands on dry ground. A dog will retrieve these birds quickly. When flight is over, it will be full daylight and the flightline will have dried up. Collect your cartridge cases, tidy up your hide area, and take your birds home and hang them in the larder.

As in all sorts of rough shooting it does not do to overshoot. Wildfowl are more than capable of looking after themselves, but there are occasions when due to weather conditions, hunger, a recent migration of unsophisticated birds or whatever, both duck and geese can be incredibly easy to shoot.

At such times restraint is the watchword. To take advantage of wildfowl which have for whatever reason dropped their guard, is not to behave in a sporting manner: who wants a sackful of dead geese and what possible pleasure can there be in amassing a heap of the slain? Once the sporting challenge has been met and a bag made it proves nothing worth proving to keep on shooting. Dreadful tales of greed abound, and it is a matter for shame that this should be the case for it plays straight into the hands of those opposed to field sports.

So much for the sermon! Such times happen rarely enough in a shooter's life but when they do he will recognise them instantly and know what to do.

Mallards will sometimes move during the day, especially when the weather is rough. The birds will fly from here to there seeking shelter and as the wind rises they move from the buffeting to places of calm. This is especially the case with river valleys, the Ouse Washes or coastal marshes. Also on the coast it is possible for a tide which rises during the day to push the wildfowl off their resting sandbar and cause them to seek another sanctuary. Good shooting may be had by someone who is aware of what is going on and who can set out a few decoys in the right place. A small, sheltered patch of water in the vicinity of the main roost or under the flightline is the favourite for a day flight.

Sometimes mallard will return from feeding to a pond or the marsh to wash their paddles and beaks after grubbing about on some muddy 'tatty bottom' and here again good sport may be had, especially under the moon. Moonflighting is part of the cream of the sport, for it is possible only when the moon is thinly veiled in cloud to provide a backdrop against which to see the birds. Being out on a dark, windy night, all alone on a desolate salting or freshwater marsh remains a great thrill in an age of over-civilisation. Thus the right combination of wind, weather, moon, tide and food can produce suitable conditions for flighting mallard and other duck, and the wildfowler must be sensitive to the signs. The matter of evening flighting on fed ponds is dealt with in Chapter 4.

Wigeon Unlike mallard, wigeon are practically all migratory, nesting in Russia and Iceland and flying south to our winter which even at its coldest is a good deal kinder than the winter in the frozen North they have left behind. The wigeon is a grazing duck, eating grass and young corn in preference to all else. Once its favourite food was a type of grass called *Zostera marina* (eel-grass), which grew below the high tide mark, but a disease wiped out most of it and what remains is guzzled by brent geese which leave none for their smaller cousins. The wigeon adapted to new foods and changed during a decade from an almost exclusively coastal duck to one which lived on great inland waters such as the new reservoirs and the Ouse Washes in Cambridgeshire, feeding on local corn drills to the annoyance of the local farmers.

Wigeon behave much as mallard do and feed at night, flighting out to splashes or small pools in or near their feeding grounds. Half-flooded water meadows are their favourite and the observant gunner will be down in time for evening flight, hidden by a gatepost or using a portable hide with a few decoys bobbing on the shallow water, waiting for the birds to arrive. Wigeon are conversational fowl and their silvery whistling is one of the most evocative sounds, second only to the gabbling of wild geese, that a wildfowler can hear. They certainly give warning of their approach.

As with many wildfowl, wigeon suffer when a long period of hard weather locks away their food supply and freezes the fields solid. They can take only so much of this and will either migrate to kinder climes or sit around disconsolately, scratching pathetically at the frozen snow trying to find a meal. At such times they are easy to shoot and the serious wildfowler leaves them in peace. The Department of the Environment imposes a ban on all wildfowl-shooting after a certain period of cold weather. A responsible wildfowler does not wait to be told when his quarry is suffering.

Wigeon are the bread and butter of the wildfowler, there for the taking by the opportunist who spots signs of their visits, an open invitation for him to drop what he is doing, hang on until dark and ambush them. They are not as wary as mallard so it is possible to shoot a fair bag in a night and although small ('half birds', the old game dealers called them), they are good to eat, provided they have not been on the tide for too long.

Wigeon fly straight and true but are quick enough to swing out of range if the gunner shows himself a few seconds too soon. They are not fools and the fowler needs to be a good judge of range and, as in all form of field shooting, be careful not to try long and hopeful shots which will only wound and leave a bird impossible to retrieve, for a pricked wigeon down on water will swim and dive like an otter. The true wildfowler prefers wigeon to mallard for they are truly wild, whereas a mallard might have been swimming on the local park lake an hour ago, taking bread from the tourists.

Teal I choose the teal as my third duck as it is so attractive and has a special

place in shooting hearts. Small and quick, springing like a rocket when disturbed, hard to shoot, excellent to eat, pretty in the hand and all-round charmer, the teal is a fine sporting bird. Agile, not so romantic as the wigeon, less prosaic than the mallard, the teal migrates here from overseas but also nests in the UK.

The flight shooter will often be caught by surprise by a flight of teal tearing low over his head or whiffling down at bewildering speed, twisting and turning to settle in an instant on the flood-water, only to rocket up the next moment and skim safely off out of sight. At last light he will hear them before he sees them, a silver soft 'pripppp' and then a ripping of wings and a spring of teal will zip round his head like bees and settle in the shallows among the tussocks. You have to be quick. A light game-gun, open borings and small shot are the necessaries of the teal shooter's trade. It has all the excitement of driven partridge shooting, but for teal you are muffled up against the cold and crouched in an uncomfortable hide in the quarter-light with the makings of a blizzard, so you are working at a disadvantage.

Add a stiff wind to the equation and teal will give you the sport of kings. Some ponds are favoured by teal just as others are preferred by mallard, so a teal pond lightly shot will provide you with a run of opportunities, but in so many varied ways do they arrive that you are never allowed to get your eye in. Two teal flights stick in my mind. One was on a wild Fen pond with a shallow skimming of water over a four-foot-deep mud pan. The birds came from over the river and a bloodshot, wild evening sky, zipped round the pond and looked to land. My, but it was classy shooting and my companion, Will Garfit the artist, and I picked up thirty-five teal between us. We lost not a bird, due to the 'A'-level work of two experienced labradors.

The other was an evening on the side of Loch Leven in Scotland, a place which sadly is shot no more as it has fallen into the hands of the

**A Canada goose is a large mouthful, even for
a labrador**

conservationists from whose grasp no shoot ever returns, so that is another
fine place lost. With a few chums, including my host Allan Allison, the
renowned taxidermist of Kinross, we waited in palatial butts round a pond
and killed some nineteen teal which came whipping in over the scrub oaks,
seen at the last minute in the gloom, and needing an instinctive swing and
snap shot to bring one down.

At other times teal pop up here and there, now and then: here sprung
from a little dyke or burn thought previously to be barren, there caught as
they swoop low over the water and taken with a true wildfowler's shot as
they pass; now mixed in with stubbling mallard in September, then
skimming the tideline racing their reflections as they twist along. The main
thing to remember about teal is—dull they ain't!

Divers Pochard and tufted duck are typical of the divers which will
feature in the bag occasionally. Designed by nature for living and feeding on
large, deep waters, their legs are set far back in their bodies for diving to the
deeps, as opposed to mallard and teal which dibble in the shallows. They fly
in a straight line with rapid wing-beats and the beat of their pinions at night
sounds harsh and rasping. The rough shooter will usually happen on a small
party of them flying along a river at midday and manage to knock one down

as they rattle past, steady as a constellation. He will see them far more often speckling the bosom of the local reservoir whence no power on earth seems capable of shifting them. As in the case of all wildfowl and all shootable birds he needs to learn to tell one from another, for not all are fair quarry.

Wild Geese

I divide this brief guide into two main sections, the truly wild grey migratory geese, of which the pink-footed and the greylag are the principle shootable members, and the feral Canada goose which has enjoyed a population explosion during the last twenty years, to the delight of shooters and the despair of farmers trying to grow cereal crops in goose areas. Some greylag geese also are termed feral, which means they are descended from domesticated stock and have taken to a life in the wild, possibly many generations ago, so that to all intents and purposes they act and behave like wild birds but do not migrate in autumn. In the winter, when the migratory greylags have arrived, the two strains are virtually indistinguishable.

The Canada goose, which is a native bird of the great American flyways where waterfowlers nickname it the Honker, started life in the UK as an ornamental bird on park lakes and there it may still be found. The creation of many gravel pits to produce raw materials for wartime aerodromes and new roads, plus the digging of ponds and lakes for trout fishing and duck shooting which in turn coincided with an increase in cereal crops, created a Canada goose paradise. Staunch defenders of their territories, even being known to drive off a fox at nesting time, the Canada proved to be what is called a 'good doer'. As it bred successfully, new breeding pairs were pushed out of the old homestead to find a place of their own; in turn they settled on new waters and fresh colonies were formed.

Feeding on corn, grass, stubbles and old potato ground, they fly from a roosting lake in the morning and spend the day out in the middle of a large field where it is difficult to come up to them. Like all geese Canadas are very wary and sharp-sighted. Usually there is at least one of a feeding gaggle with its head up alert for danger. To stalk them is, in my opinion, an acceptable practice, for anyone who belly-crawls along the broken ground, through mud and thistles until the remote opportunity arrives and he finds himself within range, is fully deserving of a shot. In the case of grey geese, though, this practice can have the effect of driving them away from that field for a very long time, possibly the rest of the season.

More conventional is to flight the birds as they arrive and depart at the feed or the roost, ambushing them from some distance away as they pass over. It is an exciting thing to see a great skein of any geese, Canadas included, on the wing beating out of an apple-green dawn, all crying and babbling their wild music. It is a sight and sound which has thrilled wildfowlers since the days of the bow and arrow.

There are two popular ways of shooting geese: one is to ambush them as they flight to feed or to roost; the other is to wait on their feeding grounds with decoys and calls, and shoot as they come in unsuspectingly. There used to be a third way, which was to dig-in or hide on their roosting grounds so that the birds would beat out wearily after a hard day spent feeding and avoiding enemies only to find that a dastardly fowler had crept out onto the mud and dug himself a shallow grave in the very middle of the roosting sandbar, whence he leaped to shoot with deadly effect into their dense ranks. They could not take that sort of punishment for long and it proved to be a sure way of causing geese to desert a whole stretch of coastline.

Wells-next-the-Sea in Norfolk was a case in point. At the turn of the century it was a haven for countless thousands of grey geese which flew in to Holkham marshes every morning and back out to the sandbars at night. An army of fowlers, including visiting gentleman gunner and ragged, local professional, assembled under the flightline with formidable fire power, anything less than an eight-bore deemed a waste of time. The birds climbed ever higher and higher on successive mornings but bigger shot, longer barrels and even mightier ordinance claimed the occasional victim, sometimes from the very High Street of Wells itself. The end came when the great birds were shot at not only on the feed but also on the roost so that they had no peace. Only then did they begin to take up other winter quarters where they were not quite so vulnerable.

In the days when the great Sam Bone was the uncrowned king of the Wells guides, all boasted of the great range and killing power of the mighty fowling-pieces. One chap even turned up with a single-barrelled, muzzle-loading two-bore with a hole drilled in the stock so that it could be used as a miniature punt gun. Its proud owner loaded it with a goodly scoop of black powder, newspaper wadding and any number of ounces of BB shot.

He would gladly lend it to any visitor who cast envious eyes upon it and begged for a shot, and would watch as they were knocked head over heels off the sea wall. People used to say it was one of the sights of Wells but the borrower would discover the hard way that one shot was enough, more than enough in fact, and rarely came back for a second go. The aspiring gunner would heave aloft this monster as the first skein approached, no matter how high. There would be a flame like a blowtorch, a deep boom and dense cloud of grey smoke and the gunner would stagger back into the road to the delight of the spectators. The great four-bore was most popular, far too large and heavy for accurate shooting, but sometimes a goose would fall from the clouds 'like a hat falling from an aeroplane'.

All this was, of course, stuff and nonsense. The power of the large-bore guns was largely a myth. Their much vaunted range was in fact little better than a twelve-bore Magnum and they were heavy to carry and swing. Their only real benefit lay in a greatly improved pattern of large shot at reasonable range which meant fewer lost and wounded birds at normal-to-long range.

The secret of shooting wildfowl, as with most sorts of quarry, is to get close enough to be sure of a clean kill, and having done so, to use open borings and small shot which produce good patterns, lots and lots of pellets in that critical thirty-inch circle.

The hardest part is the first, finding good range, and to that end are the various subterfuges and snares of the fowler, the hiding in creeks on cold mornings so that the birds might be caught unawares, the use of decoys to

Decoys improve the chances of the fowler

Left:
A well-established butt will pay dividends

Top:
The spaniel is good in water

Above:
A bird in the hand

A good drake mallard is quite a mouthful

draw them in, the call to deceive them, and the taking advantage of gales of wind which might cause them to lose height by a vital few yards. Once you have used the real skills of field-craft to get close enough to kill and not to wound, the rest is easy and may be learned on a clay-ground in an hour by a moderately receptive pupil.

Geese feed by day and roost at night, but sometimes they will feed along with other wildfowl under the moon and as with wigeon, moonflighting is one of the most thrilling elements of wildfowl shooting. Geese will fly lower in a head wind, in fog, a blizzard or any conditions which unsettle them and put them at a disadvantage.

Geese fly much faster than they appear to do. One used to shooting pheasants or other wildfowl will have to make allowances for the beating of those great wings which, although apparently slow and cumbersome, make it one of the fastest birds that fly. Due allowance must be made to shoot at head and neck and firmly shut out all thoughts of that great body and canopy pinions. Geese on the shoreline are the purist's birds shot in the old way at good range as they pass over; it is unlikely that a large bag can ever be made in such circumstances. Geese on the feeding fields can be a very different matter.

By finding the right field, a simple matter of reconnaissance, begging permission, a far less simple matter, and hiding carefully on the upwind side of the field with a handful of decoys placed, you should find that the geese set their wings and come straight for the decoys, provided their sharp eyes do not detect anything untoward in your 'picture' or your concealment. There is that old thrill of the calling as they draw near, that moment of decision as to whether or not they are in range (always a hard matter for the novice to judge, for geese are large birds), the slow rise for the shot, the careful aim and swing and the moment of fierce elation as a bird falls.

It pays to watch the skein as it flies off, even if you feel you have registered a complete miss, for more often than you might think a bird will peel out and fall dead sometimes half a mile away, the result of a pellet in heart or lung, or maybe more than one, for geese are strong birds, built to cross great oceans and weather mighty storms, and they take a deal of stopping.

However, when all goes according to plan and none of the many things which can go wrong do go wrong, it is all too easy to shoot an excessively large bag on the fields over decoys. The rough shooter's creed is to see that all he shoots is eaten, if not by him then by someone else, and a huge pile of geese, greys or Canadas, does no one any good. I made the point in my remarks about duck shooting and for no logical reason the crime of greed seems so much blacker in the case of geese.

We are illogical people; we swat a fly without a thought and castigate a man who wantonly kills a butterfly; the mildest-mannered housewife sets a trap in the pantry for a rat but writes to the paper in indignation if she sees someone shoot its close relation, a grey squirrel. To shoot a great number of geese is not a matter of which to be proud for we all know that they can be as painfully easy as they can be impossibly difficult to shoot. You are not allowed by law to sell excess bags, and tales abound of greedy fowlers burying piles of the slain or heaping them in the nearest ditch for the farmer to find—well—draw your own conclusions. Such a noble bird deserves better. In my opinion, half a dozen at a flight is more than enough for one gun to shoot.

Waders

The golden plover, snipe and woodcock are the main quarry species in this category. Time was when the list was a good deal longer and as recently as the Wildlife and Countryside Act of 1981 it included curlew and redshank, but these birds too were removed from the list of quarry species which has been whittled away a shaving at a time during the last half-century. In the old days a 'longshore gunner' would come home with a mixed bag of waders which his missus would boil up in a great pudding along with any other scraps of meat she had handy and create an oystercock pie. No two were identical in flavour because the ingredients varied, but along with many of the other old practices of the lonely gunners, the dish is a thing of the past.

Today only three remain. *The golden plover* is not shot much these days but it is a real rough shooter's bird for all that, good to eat and exciting to shoot, found on the high moorland, lowground stubbles or the saltmarsh. It is a restless bird, here today and who knows where next week. It delays in its migration, having certain favourite fields which it tends to use year after year. The passing driver will see the field dotted with birds, pull into the next layby and wind down his window to hear the familiar double whistle.

A pretty bird, the goldie, of speckled gold with black underparts, fading to more uniform browns in winter, with its three-toed, upright stance; often standing mixed with peewits all facing the wind like a parade of grenadiers or taking to the air and skimming round in formation, changing direction all as one with bewildering aerial evolutions. At other times it flies low along the tideline. Flight shooting can be very exciting with goldies seeming almost to drop vertically from the heavens. On coastal marshes goldies flight inland at dawn (like geese) and out again at sunset. Later in the season they form large flocks on splashy meadows and river washes, often associating with peewits on the ground but not flying with them.

The future of this species looks doubtful as a sporting proposition. It is on the shooting list for what can only be quirky reasons, for what the fowler considered to be, the equally populous and desirable curlew and redshank were, as I have explained, excluded. I try to be an optimist but have little doubt that in time the goldie will be added to the list of lost quarry, a step supported by no scientific evidence, for some 30,000 pairs breed here and about half a million of them winter here and in Ireland. Few are shot each year and the bird seems to be more than holding its own, although its range moves slightly further north for climatic reasons. The rough shooter will be poorer if and when the golden plover is taken from him.

The snipe too is far from safe from the legislators. Far better known than the

Opposite:
Fenland idyll: two labradors, an eight-bore and a pinkfoot

goldie, with its long probing bill, zigzag flight and legendary hardness as a sporting target, the snipe is well known even by those who may never have seen one. The common snipe (as opposed to the smaller, rarer and protected jack snipe) breeds virtually throughout the northern hemisphere. It requires damp marshy places with suitable cover for feeding and nesting. One of the problems with declining numbers in the UK has been caused by the systematic drainage of snipe marshes for agricultural reasons.

Snipe tend to feed at night but the rough shooter will be aware of one when, with the utmost suddenness, it springs from the rushes almost at his feet with a harsh 'scaaaap' of alarm and sets off twisting and turning in an evasive way until it is out of range. Some schools of thought believe in firing immediately and hoping the snap shot will score, others wait until the third twist whereafter they claim that the flight levels out and the target is more easy. I have never found this to work, for usually the bird is well out of range by the time it has stopped twisting, while as for the three turns rule, nobody seems to have told my snipe about it.

There is further debate about whether to walk the birds upwind or downwind. The upwind school maintains that the keen hearing of the birds is nullified and the gunner gets a closer range shot, whereas the downwind school holds that the bird will, like all birds, rise into the wind, and might give a passing shot as it comes back through the guns. Snipe lie singly, sometimes in small groups called wisps but rarely in larger flocks.

Snipe are usually shot walked up, but there are some places where they lend themselves to being driven. The guns stand in a line of butts across the marsh and the beaters will come in from a distance, splashing across the shallows for all the world like beaters on a partridge shoot. The snipe will flush easily and fly very high over the guns, their initial twisting long over, but still slanting across the sky and difficult to hit. There is such a snipe drive on Anglesey where I have been privileged to shoot and another connected with a famous fishing inn in Devon.

The snipe being a small bird it is often a problem to judge range, and when the bird appears to be quite a small dot against the clouds it is closer than you imagine. At long range there is a risk of the bird passing through the pattern of game shot although it takes only a single pellet to knock one down. However, in my experience far more snipe pass *round* the pattern than through it!

The rough shooter will come to know where a snipe might lie and when he feels the ground growing soft and splashy beneath his feet he will be at the ready for a quick shot. Shooting men and enlightened farmers do what they can to preserve the marshy habitat and some vital areas have had protection orders slapped upon them to prevent drainage. All sportsmen hope that such measures have been taken in time and that the snipe does not find itself added to the dreaded 'deleted' list of shootable gamebirds.

Two final thoughts: first, the favourite breakfast of Sir Winston Churchill was a couple of snipe on toast washed down with champagne, and second, some Irish snipe shooters of the past entered folklore with their consistent performance at this difficult bird. They developed a special knack over many years of practice and would kill bird after bird with the most astonishing consistency. I suspect that like oystercock pie, such giants too are things of the past, for today neither the desire nor the opportunity to become a champion snipe shot have survived.

The woodcock is the third and possibly most famous of the wader family although, like the snipe, you need a game licence to shoot one. This is a bird overcharged with excitement and the cry of 'Cock forward!' on shooting day has the shooter flourishing his gun and looking round eagerly, a danger

signal to all and sundry, while the spectators and beaters hurl themselves face down on the ground. Normally safe and sane folk behave oddly when a 'cock' is up. In the old days farm lads would catch them in horsehair nooses and sell them to the gentry, for the birds were easy to guide by means of little fences of twigs into the traps. This gave it the reputation for foolishness and its name became synonymous with stupidity.

The rounded wings and moth-like flight, the long beak carried at a downward angle, the sudden sideways flick and the lack of any apparent reaction to being shot at are all give-aways of this magical bird. It feeds mainly at night and spends the day in the bottom of old oak woods, in rhododendrons, little spinneys or by muddy streams where there is soft mud and cover in which to hide. It will spring aloft with an electric whirring of wings and throw itself sideways across the glade; tantalisingly slow, it seems, an easy shot, but as it tops the silver birches it has you contemplating two wasted cartridges and gazing ruefully after its departure.

Apart from its generally unusual appearance it has great black eyes set far up in its head and designed by nature so that it can see through 360 degrees, making it impossible to approach unseen; it can feed and watch out for danger at the same time. With its short legs and long bill (probably evolved after the wading habit diminished), the woodcock has the curious habit of carrying its chicks away from danger by flying off with them clutched between its thighs. This was one of the famous old debating points where

Opposite:
A right and a left at woodcock is a rarely achieved feat

62

two or more shooting men were gathered together but it has been witnessed by so many reliable people (although never yet photographed) that now the phenomenon is accepted as fact.

Like the snipe, the woodcock possesses at the end of each wing tip, and alongside the quill of the first primary, a short sharp spiky feather a little over an inch long and called a pin-feather. This is a corruption of 'pen' feather for in the early days the tiny quill was highly prized by artists who used it for drawing fine lines. Now, as a pin-feather, it is treasured only by him who is fortunate enough to shoot the woodcock, and with loving care he sticks them into his game-book, sets them in his hatband or puts them in a special brooch made to accommodate them. The grandmother of Lord Margadale was said to have possessed a fan made from no less than 10,000 woodcock pin-feathers.

So difficult is the bird to shoot that a special Club was formed for those who had killed a right-and-left at woodcock—that is, two consecutive birds in two shots, seen simultaneously and in front of two witnesses. This Club is administered by the *Shooting Times* magazine and winners are entitled to wear a badge and tie, attend an annual dinner and be presented with a special bottle of whisky. Much can go wrong so membership is exclusive. The second bird is missed, there are no witnesses, one of the birds is shared

by another gun, one of the two downed is not retrieved—the life of a right-and-left-er at woodcock is full of such anxieties.

Many woodcock are shot on pheasant shoots, but the rough shooter who comes home with a 'ditch owl' in the bag is a lucky man with every right to feel proud. The bird lends itself to the opportunist approach of the rough

shooter for it is here today and gone tomorrow. There is an old saying that the time to shoot woodcock is when you see them, for by tomorrow they will have gone, migrating as they do ever westwards until they end up on the west coast of Ireland or the furthest tip of Cornwall.

The bird is doing well, and Game Conservancy figures indicate a steady annual increase, one of the few wild gamebirds of which that claim might be made. The planting of more broadleaved woodlands (the result of public opinion fed up with blanket afforestation and the creation of barren miles of green conifers) will ensure that the all-important good woodcock habitat remains available.

Usually the woodcock will be regarded by the rough shooter as an incidental, a surprise bonus on a day after pheasants or rabbits. In the West Country and Wales this is not the case for there the woodcock densities are high enough for them to be the main quarry species; wild pheasants are correspondingly thin on the ground. The long narrow woodlands of those parts with their strips of holly, scrub oak and birch are perfect for woodcock and also for small groups of guns walking them in the hope of a shot.

Like the pheasant, the woodcock is a bird of the boundaries, preferring to land in a clearing and walk into cover. Thus the wise shooter will work the rides, field boundaries and edges of the dense woodland. A questing dog working either side of a ride will flush the birds and you would be surprised at how often they choose to fly down or across the ride in which you stand. Generally speaking, woodcock need little flushing, although there are some specialists who use one of the pointing breeds which will hold the quarry until the shooter is ready for action. This in turn makes for problems caused by working in thick cover, the solution found by our Continental cousins being to tie a small bell round the neck of the dog so that its position in the rough can be established. When the bell falls silent the dog is presumably on point and it is as well that at least someone in the party knows roughly where it was working prior to that all-important moment.

As in most forms of rough shooting, little extemporary drives may be arranged. The woodcock does not lend itself to being driven as usually it goes where it likes rather than where you want it. However, the beating-out of a small spinney for a 'cock' is worth a try; bearing in mind that the drive should be short, for it is not often that a 'cock' will fly more than two or three hundred yards without settling, and that there is the risk of the bird breaking back. Woodcock coming forward will fly through rather than over the trees so care with safety must be a priority and there will be no high-flying 'scorchers' to deal with.

Another method is to flight woodcock. Quite by chance I discovered that my own little flight pond is on one of those flightlines which it is so hard to discover. The birds roost during the day and in the evening flight out to the plashy water meadows and farmland to feed. They get into the habit of using the same corridors for this purpose year after year. Many times, when duck flighting, I regularly saw woodcock fly past always coming from the same direction and heading for the same destination. Never did I get a chance for a shot, as I was thinking duck, and by the time I had made a positive identification, the moment was past. And although I have found this flightline, only one woodcock has been shot from it and that by my son Peter who, being young and quick, has sharper reactions than his old man.

My view is that such a flightline can be over-exploited, especially in country where woodcock are scarce. If half a dozen birds use it it will not take long for them to be shot by a line of guns waiting for them to arrive. To take the odd one is one thing, to set out to over-capitalise on a stroke of luck is quite another. If you have been caning the birds by walking them up during the day and thereafter you systematically ambush them on a flightline you are at risk of making serious inroads into a non-replenishable stock.

Pigeons

Later in this book I will be explaining in more detail about the mysteries of pigeon decoying, one of the great arts in shooting sports and popular in its own right. The woodpigeon is a fine sporting bird and to the rough shooter it could be his bread and butter, bag-filler and consolation on an otherwise blank day. There are none of the problems or agonising associated with snipe, woodcock or grey partridge shooting; this bird is common, a good breeder, an agricultural pest which thrives despite the worst that Man can throw at it. The pigeon, like the rabbit, may be shot without compunction at any time.

BUT—and there is so often a *but* in shooting matters—there is a slight question mark in some minds about shooting in high summer when the bird you kill might well have squabs on the nest. This is one of the old moral questions which may be fairly applied to the shooting of all so-called pest species in the breeding season. I make no judgement upon it here, it is up to the individual to decide for himself and act accordingly.

The pigeon is used to being number one enemy of the farmer and it is well versed in the art of looking after itself. No pigeon will fly over a man in the open if it has seen him first; and its eyesight is so razor-sharp that the chances of its not seeing him are remote. Disturbed from the thickets, trees or the most impenetrable thorn-bush it flies out on the far side, giving you no chance of a shot. It flies high and fast, jinking at the first sign of trouble from below. It feeds spasmodically and unpredictably (time was when the opposites were the case), and it is in every way a sporting bird. Not being a farmer I cannot regard it as vermin and I hold a great respect and admiration for a bird which has given me so much good sport in so many places over so many years.

The rough shooter will see the pigeon as a bird to be decoyed (see Chapter 3), a target for shooting as it lands in the roosting woods at night or a bird to be snap shot as it blunders from the aforementioned bush or flies high across and misjudges the range as you plod your way. Like woodcock, pigeons may also be flighted if you can intercept a line from the feeding areas to the roosting woods.

This can be exciting shooting; I know because we have such a place on our little shoot in the Fens. The pigeons funnel in from a vast area and follow the lines of straggling spinneys and shelter belts, working their way up to the higher wooded ground in the villages on the edge of the Suffolk Downs. Crossing that line is a handy ditch where a man can hide in comfort and, gazing in the right direction, see flight upon flight of pigeons in wavering lines, rising and falling, approaching his position. Such flightlines, and ours is no exception, are often on too wide a front for one man to cover effectively, but two or three guns can have a magnificent evening's sport provided there is a wind stiff enough to bring the birds down to within range.

Not everyone has access to such a place, in which case a good second-best is what is known as roost shooting. For this, the gun hides in the clump of trees in which the pigeons roost every winter evening. The clump can be anything from a huge wood to a tiny stand of conifers. No matter what the birds have been doing during the day they will flight in at last light to these same places and it is a poor sort of wood which has no pigeon flightline whatever.

Arriving within a couple of hours of darkness the gun hides near an opening in the canopy and bides his time. Early pigeons will be tempting as they arrow across the sky and present fleeting, extreme range chances but the urge to have snap shots at such passing opportunities must be resisted. Wait until the bird is committed to landing and is in good range. Firing too early at high and hopeless flocks does no more than waste ammunition and scare the birds for later when they might come in more kindly.

Some find it hard to shoot through a frieze of twigs and there is no doubt that the smallest stick can knock great holes in your pattern. The trick here is

to shoot as though you were in the open; try and ignore the obstructions and swing through in the normal way. You will hit many more in that way than by attempting to snap shoot them as they cross the gaps. This shooting provides a great variety of targets, from simple ones which flop along at tree-top level to high curlers and birds which close their wings and drop from an enormous height to settle in the topmost branches. As in most flight shooting, high winds are favoured conditions and calm nights the worst. Who needs driven pheasant shooting when they have good pigeon roost shooting available? It is a good deal cheaper, gives you more shots and a greater variety of chances.

Pigeons may be happened on at almost any time when out shooting. In the summer they will sit in thorn hedges or elders and clatter out as you walk past. The pigeon escape trick of emerging always on the opposite side can be counteracted by having a companion who will walk along the far side so that the bird has no safe escape route. A number of young birds may be shot this way and the squabs are the most delicious eating, especially with redcurrant jelly.

Feral pigeons are also fair game but racing pigeons are strictly protected. Telling them apart is not easy even for experts. The native stockdove and rock dove are protected, as is the migratory turtle dove, the voice of the English summer with its delicate crooning on warm afternoons. The most recent immigrant, the collard dove, is the only bird to have been put *onto* the list of shootable birds for many a long year. Its colonisation of this country from eastern Europe was one of the phenomenons of the sixties, prior to which the bird was a very rare migrant. I shot one of the first seen in Cambridgeshire and had it stuffed at considerable expense, a tribute to its rarity. Little was I to know that within five years there would be a pair in every suburban garden.

It is not a contender for serious consideration on the shooter's list but specialised sport of good quality may be had round barns and farmyards where the birds gather in great numbers, especially when grain is stored. The collared dove is not a bird of the open fields like the woodpigeon. A few minutes' pretty shooting may be enjoyed before the birds clear off and then if you wait they will come trickling back. Collared doves are good to eat, feeding always on the choicest foods and invariably in excellent condition. The protected turtle dove is superficially similar, so the aspiring collared dove shooter must be sure of his identification. The turtle dove has a heavily marked chestnut-brown back and a darker tail; unless you can tell the difference, the golden rule as with all shooting is, do not fire.

Of every hundred pigeons shot in the UK ninety-nine are shot over decoys, a matter to which I will be returning in great depth later on.

Ground Game

Rabbits and hares form the two main components of this category, although some rough shooters grow excited about shooting and eating grey squirrels and pronounce them tasty. This is surely a peripheral matter and not one to cover in depth—if indeed there is any depth to cover.

An 'easy' hare is easy to miss

Hares may be shot in stubbles or fields of roots or, in the case of the blue or mountain hare, on the heather moorlands and cotton-grass hillsides. A hare is up and away when the gun approaches, so it needs no flushing and dogs ought to be at heel if you are expecting a shot. A hare will sit in its form on sometimes quite open arable land in which case it is harder to approach than in thicker country. This is a very fair mark and proper quarry for the rough shooter and although the brown hare has suffered mixed fortunes lately and has become thin on the ground in some areas, it is still common enough in others. It is a swift runner and a going-away shot is liable to wound unless taken at good range, so no long shots please. Nothing is more pitiful than the sight and sound of a wounded hare making off, still too fast for a hunting dog and doomed to an awful end.

When driving hares or rabbits it is best for the walkers to work downwind. There are some parts of the country where the traditional hare shoot takes place. Although 'puss' has fallen on hard times in a general sense there are pockets where concentrations of them are such that they constitute an agricultural menace by nibbling sugar-beet and corn and become prone to the diseases associated with too dense populations. Such places often fall within the eastern counties of England where the wide arable acres are suited to hares. The hare shoot was often the perk of locals known to be rough shooters, wildfowlers and pigeon men, and sadly the events became synonymous with dangerous shooting to the extent that the older hands would not go within a mile of one.

With ground game dodging past unprotected ankles, it needed only one

inexperienced or over-eager gun in the field and the risk of ricochets from flints and other accidents became rife. I was in Gallyon's gun shop in Cambridge one day some years ago and a green wellington boot as full of holes as a colander was produced as silent witness to the dangers inherent in free-for-all hare shoots. On some of them there would be more than a hundred armed men and a bag of hares which ran into the hundreds.

Nothing wrong with a hare shoot, provided the stocks warrant a cull and you know the track record, proven experience and safety of other people who are likely to be present. All hares should be shot at a maximum of thirty yards' range and shot should be no smaller than number four. Hares may be killed by smaller pellets but best to take no chances. Watch a hit hare out of sight; many times it will run on and then suddenly keel over.

For the walking rough shooter it is worth remembering that a good brown hare can tip the scales at about seven pounds weight. Shoot three of them and carry them for the whole of a hot September day and you will have an aching shoulder. Make sure that if you shoot a hare you are happy first to carry it, and second to eat it. Neither course is to everyone's taste any more. Worst of all is to have a running-in dog who rushes in to shot and retrieves hares shot by others. The wretched animal brings back a mighty hare which your neighbour has bowled over, just as you are about to tackle a stiff climb up the moor to grouse country. It is not always convenient to plod over to the man and hand it to him, not for the shy and inexperienced maybe; but being neither, I never fail to pass it on to its rightful owner.

Rabbits The rabbit is the rough shooter's speciality, one shootable creature he does not share with the driven game shot. Time was when everyone

Overleaf:
Ferret entered; guns at the ready

learned to shoot at rabbits; that was before the advent of myxomatosis, when the great warrens offered sport at rabbits as they nipped from hole to hole or across wooded rides, pushed out by ferret or terrier. Many a labouring family was kept alive by rabbits and during the war the whole country fed on them. A special train, The Rabbit Train, ran from Norfolk to London twice weekly with wagon after wagonload of Norfolk rabbits to feed the hungry folk in the big city.

Brought here by Roman or Norman, highly valued for their fur and meat, farmed commercially right up to the end of the last century, natural survivor and universal feeder of both man and a whole succession of winged and four-footed predators, the rabbit has become an integral part of the country scene. A formidable breeder, a single pair in ideal conditions being said to be able in theory to establish a colony of a million in twelve months, the bunny is a godsend to the rough shooter.

Since the scourge of the disease, rabbits have changed their habits and in

some areas have made a return to strength of something approaching the best (or worst, depending on whether you are a farmer) of the old pre-myxy days. Rather than living in concentrated colonies and huge warrens where the deadly rabbit flea which transmitted the disease could move freely round a great number of hosts, the rabbit now lives in more scattered colonies, sometimes above ground, in cracks in dry banks, under jumbled heaps of concrete and in bushes. On my little duck marsh a colony of rabbits has appeared from nowhere and lives and loves very happily in a series of huge fissures in the ground caused when the soil dried out in a very dry summer.

Good sport may be had with a .22 rifle or high-powered air weapon, but as this book is concerned primarily with shotgunning we leave that matter for another day. Rabbits will lie out rough in tussocky fields and on stubbles in good weather. An old trick was to leave Renardine or some other noxious stuff in the burrows the night before shooting: this would cause the rabbits to lie out rather than face the stench and consequently they would be out in sufficient numbers to provide sport.

Shooting rabbits as they bolt from a warm seat in the sunshine and scuttle into the hedge is an acquired art calling for a swift rise and shoot with good forward allowance. Bolting rabbit is now an event at many sporting clay pigeon shoots and it provides a chance for the rough shooter to brush up his skills for the real thing. As with all ground game shooting, special care must be taken with safety and the old adage about never shooting where you cannot see is especially apt. A rabbit running alongside a hedge might just be in line with the leg of a person unseen on the other side or might be hotly pursued by a dog concealed from the shooter by broken ground. Rabbit shooting can be accident-prone unless you are very careful.

Cream of the sport is when you happen on a set of holes in the middle of an open field. This is the time for the ferret to be called into action; slip him in and stand back. The idea is that the rabbits will be pushed out and dash for the safety of the hedgerow or field edge and provide cracking shots.

Ferreting traditionally is done with nets whereby the sportsman places purse nets over all holes before slipping in the ferret. This results in clean (ie un-shot-damaged) rabbits which are greatly preferred by the kitchen staff to shot ones. However, the sportsman would rather take an exciting running shot than content himself only with supplying the larder. For all use of ferrets the approach to the holes should be made silently with no thumping on the ground, no approaching from an upwind direction, and no shouting or smoking. If the rabbits know you are there they will face the ferret or simply slip from the mouth of one hole to another without giving you a chance.

There are many good books on ferreting, a subject which lies beyond the scope of this one, but many rough shooters taking up the gentle art come to prefer it almost to any other form of opportunist, do-it-yourself rough shooting. Try it, and you will see why, and with the rabbit returning in such numbers to the British countryside, the future of this sport is encouraging.

Oddments

Any animal or bird which is not on the protected list or has an open season may be considered a fair mark for the rough shooter; he tends not to be a fussy individual about such matters. Every crow foolish enough to beat over his head as he waits in a hide, the magpie slipping out of the high thorn-hedge or even a rat surprised as it shuffles up to no good along the foot of the bank is worth a shot. All such may be termed enemies of game and they may be shot at any time. In some parts of the country crow and rook shooting has become a sport in its own right. A decoy may be set out and shooting can be steady. An old trick was to put a live ferret or tame owl out in a field; this would attract the inquisitive corvids to mob it and again a great many could be shot. This dodge might fall foul of the tethering-a-live-decoy legislation, but it has yet to be tested.

Corvids roost in favoured woods and, like pigeons, will flight in at last light with a great cawing and palaver before settling down. A gun waiting in the wood can have good sport with them and every one killed helps the keeper and improves the prospects of the wild game. The driven game shooter would be unlikely to waste a cartridge on a passing head of vermin and if he does so, does it with some distaste. Not so the rough shooter who takes every chance he can.

Young rooks were traditionally shot in the first week of May when the squabs clung to the topmost branches with their scaly feet. It was held that the rook was a farming pest, a view now disputed by evidence which

suggests that the rook does as much if not more good than harm by eating great numbers of troublesome insects such as wireworms. The rook shoot was not much of a sporting occasion, for the young rooks would not fly but allowed themselves to be shot down tamely with rifles or shotguns while the old birds wheeled around anxiously overhead. This is not a common practice these days, for which I am not sorry, as I rather like the rook, a symbol of the English ploughland, like Mr Pickwick and roast beef and the late lamented ancient elms, a vital part of village life. The carrion crow with its pickaxe beak and cruel ways is another matter altogether.

All corvids are enemies of game

Another shootable bird which is underrated is the moorhen. This marsh dweller is less innocent than it looks, with its habit of egg-stealing from duck and pheasant nests, robbing corn left for gamebirds, or aggressively defending a territory against more desirable candidates: it is also good to eat. Moorhens do not often present sporting targets and their habit when surprised is to skitter low on the water to the far rushes where they dive and hide, or fly tamely up to sit in a thicket and look at you—that is if you can get them to flush at all. There are odd days in a gale of wind when a moorhen will rise in its teeth and go soaring high like a blown, black rag. That is more like it, but most of the time it is an easy target, although like many easy targets, it can be surprisingly easy to miss. People tend to shoot in front of it or 'poke' at it.

The moorhen really scores on the table, where it can be mixed with a bit of kidney and made into a passable substitute for steak in a pie. No fingers may pluck the fine 'dowl' or fluff with which its body is covered, but skin it in a few seconds and, provided you have enough of them, you have the traditional marshman's supper, and very good it is. Too many moorhens are wasted or fed to ferrets. Remember the old rule: if you cannot eat it, or if it is not a pest species which conflicts with your interests, then it should not be shot.

Thus a brief Who's Who and What's What of the quarry species which the rough shooter might reasonably expect to encounter. His days are less structured and formal than those of the game shooter, his room for error is greater. There is a common view that driven game shooting is harder than rough shooting; I do not subscribe to it. In the latter the decisions, plans, tactics, safety, game-cart and so on are all in the hands of the shooter; he is keeper, beater, picker-up, dog handler, shoot captain and bag-carrier.

The risk he suffers is that of overshooting, especially wild pheasants on unkeepered farmland. There are those who comb the fields every Saturday accompanied by mongrel dogs, shoot hens and cocks as they rise, right up into the end of the season. This is greed, one of the curses of the age. Being left to his own devices the rough shooter must add to his other responsibilities that of conserving the stocks on his ground.

It would be good to think that there will be something there for his son and grandson to shoot at after he has gone.

3
Pigeon Shooting

'I still can't understand how I missed that last one!'

Often considered—and quite wrongly so—as a poor man's sport, the shooting of pigeons over decoys is in my view one of the great arts of country shooting sports. It is tailor-made for the rough shooter, being a sport in which he finds his own birds, plans his tactics, makes his hides, applies field-craft, shoots and carries his gear much as does the man who walks the fields in search of a pheasant or two. The pigeon is a common bird, an agricultural pest which lives in flocks, is wary and sharp-eyed, suspicious of Man and all his works and an aerial gymnast, giving it all the qualities of a worthy adversary.

Its habit of feeding in huge numbers on all the best food—one flock could run into many thousands of birds—makes it an ideal customer for the decoyer. The idea is to set up within easy range of a comfortable hide, a party of pigeon decoys set in lifelike positions to simulate a real flock. New pigeons flying into the field will see them and swoop in to join them, little knowing that you, a dangerous sentinel, are lying in wait. That is the beginning, middle and end of decoying; the refinements and tactics have become subtle and myriad but at the end of the day that is all there is to it. BUT, as with many simple things, there is much which can go wrong.

The hide might be built in the wrong place. Like every bird ever hatched, pigeons will not land downwind so your hide must be set on the downwind side of the field so that new arrivals fly towards the decoyer rather than away from him. If your decoys are unrealistic, too close together, all facing into the wind—another thing no birds care to do for long—or if you are using certain sorts of plastic ones which shine in the sun and glint in the rain, then again, nothing is likely to come your way. If your hide is made so badly that you may be seen through its leafy screen, a white face bobbing up and down like a balloon on a string with a pair of equally white hands fluttering like a pair of

81

**The lone shooter in roots; better to stay at
home than go without a dog**

Cabbage White butterflies in the shadowy recesses, no self-respecting pigeon will come within two hundred yards of you. If you … but to begin at the beginning.

Find the right field and you are halfway to making a bag; get permission to shoot upon it and you are three-quarters of the way there. Many farmers will be pleased to have someone keep the birds off a vulnerable crop at a critical time, and will be even more eager if they know you already, or if you come recommended by a mutual acquaintance. However, it is worth remembering that the old free and easy days have long gone, when farmers begged on bended knees for you to come and would provide you with free cartridges into the bargain. Pigeon shooting is in demand, some of it is let and much is in the hands of the game shooting tenant who likes to keep it for himself. You might have to knock on a door or two and suffer rebuffs before you receive the green light.

Let us say that all has gone well and you have kept a pigeon field under close surveillance for a week or so. You will have seen the birds using it in gradually increasing numbers, and seen that the crop is not one which they will clear quickly, leaving you in danger of arriving on your day off, but after the pigeon has bolted. Beans and peas are a case in point; large, obvious seeds which the birds can scoop up easily without missing any. Drilled corn takes longer and growing greenstuffs or laid corn longer still to mop up. Choosing the optimum moment, ideally a day of sun and wind after the birds have grown confident, are undisturbed and numbers have built up nicely, you make your play.

Back bent beneath the weight of your equipment, you arrive at the gateway and gaze round. A great flock rises with a clatter from the field by the far ash-poles. Do you rush there straightaway and set up? You could, and you just might get it right first time, but better restrain yourself and spend a few minutes, something like fifteen of them, really, assessing the flightlines. Your earlier reconnaissance will have given you some idea of where these aerial highways are, but check to make sure. Your aim is to attract new birds which arrive by one or more of those flightlines, so hide siting is of great importance. Get it wrong and moving is not only an awful bore but a waste of vital shooting time.

You might be tempted by a commodious elder bush not in *quite* the right place; what a super and comfortable hide it would make, hardly any need to adapt it, ready-made, in fact. Put such temptations behind you; a bad hide in the right place is ten times better than a good hide in the wrong place. Make your decision and move across the field to your chosen spot, taking care if it is a standing crop such as laid corn or peas (both pigeon favourites) that you

skirt the edge and do not trample it down. A farmer prefers the pigeon and all his works to a wandering pigeon shooter with large and clumsy feet.

Decide on the place for a hide and, using the natural formation of the branches, cut into the hedge but not in such a way as to damage it and render it no longer stock-proof; certainly do not chop and snip at hardwood saplings in your attempts to create a comfortable bower. The fronds of thorn and elder may be cut about with impunity but to damage good timber and ruin a hedge is to earn very black marks with your host. A pair of secateurs or a straight hedge-slasher is useful for hide-making and ought to be part of your kit. Bend and trim rather than cut through; a few scraps of binder string will hold back a bough so that you adapt nature to suit rather than bludgeon her, leaving a suitable gap for your head and shoulders to protrude when you stand up and room to swing and shoot with comfort.

You might use one of the commercially produced camouflage nets which hang on adjustable poles. Some of these are very good and may be set up anywhere when there is no natural cover available, but beware the ones too dark in colour. Cammo nets as cammo, clothing ought to be as light as possible to blend with the colours of a hedge or woodside. For a seat you might use an old five-gallon drum which costs nothing, or a patent, shortened shooting-stick gadget which costs quite a lot. When seated you should be able to see through the hide: do not peep over the top of the leading edge, and if you can half roof it or make sure there is a good backdrop to conceal the occupant, so much the better. Hide-making is an art at which one gets better with practice.

Next you set out your decoys. There are several good types on the market including the minimalist Shell decoys which pack one inside another for ease of carrying, or the full-bodied Sportplast models which are available almost anywhere. You need at least a dozen to start you off, and you spread them about, all roughly but not exactly facing the wind, in natural feeding positions within good range of the hide. There ought to be a generous two metres between each two, for even in the densest flock there is more space between the individual members than you might imagine. If possible leave a space into which incoming pigeons will be attracted to land, the killing area, so that you end up with a decoy picture in a U shape, a V or a comma— anything in fact which leaves an attractive open space in front of your hide where you would prefer to take your shots.

The experts prefer to use dead pigeons rather than artificials for decoys and many of the really heavy bags have been made in this way. If you shoot pigeons regularly you should carry forward a stock for next time or keep a batch in the freezer, remembering to thaw them out well in advance, then the real pigeons are more readily attracted. Dead birds may be propped up with a wire or sharp stick jabbed under their chins to hold their heads up in a natural way. Of course, as you shoot pigeons and add them to the decoy picture, either you take in the artificials as you go, or you supplement your original squad of real birds, and as your decoy pattern becomes larger it is even more attractive to new arrivals.

On drilled land the decoys may simply be placed in position on the ground but where the crop is tall you will have to set them on canes or perch them precariously on top of the fronds. Much stock is set by expert pigeon shooters on movement. It is felt that a moving decoy is much more attractive than a static one, and if the aim is to create realism then this makes sense; a flock of feeding pigeons is a whole picture of movement as the birds bob up and down and walk with their nautical, strutting gait from beakful to beakful. This is made possible with artificials by mounting them on springy wires or rocking pegs which allows them to tip and tilt in the breeze, but is harder with real birds.

Various dodges and gadgets are on the market which claim to represent a moving pigeon: wing-flappers, swoopers and a variety of curious engines and devices, all invented by practical pigeon shooters and a lot of fun to use. There is no doubt that some movement is very attractive if you can achieve it easily, but to take out too much complicated gear on a muddy day and lug it to the far side of fifty acres of heavy drilled land in the rain can defeat the object of the exercise which is, remember, to enjoy yourself.

A further refinement of decoying is to perch a few up a nearby tree. Here again the object is to show the real pigeons something they would expect to see: look at any feeding-field and sure enough, invariably there are some pigeons perched on the field-edge trees. Long aluminium poles which fix together may be used to lift a decoy until it lodges in the topmost twigs of a modest ash (always a favourite pigeon tree), and if you are prepared to go to the trouble of carrying the poles with you then this can be a useful addition to your armoury.

You will find that pigeon shooting can take a grip on its adherents so that they come to abandon all other sorts of shooting in favour of it. My purpose today is to show that it represents one of many aspects of the complete rough shooter's calendar and that he capitalises on it when it is available and turns to other elements of his sport when it is not.

Having made all of the above arrangements, and it is amazing how quickly you can do it after practice, you settle down in the hide and hope that the birds come pouring in. If you have done your homework properly and are in luck, then that is what will happen, but there is much to go wrong which is not your fault. A change in the weather, a local migration which takes the flocks to new pastures, the farmer setting up a banger to keep them off, someone else coming to shoot or simply the fickle nature of the birds themselves can all undo you, but that is the sport and the risk is part of the fun.

You will watch through and not over the hide edge, otherwise the incomers will spot your face a mile off. Wait until the pigeon is in good range and committed to landing, and rise and shoot in one smooth movement. It is a knack easily acquired by anyone with a feel for the sport. Sometimes birds will come in in twos, threes and large flocks; the trick here is to go for right-and-lefts for this is the way to build up a good bag. Take each shot one at a time; many are missed by the shooter thinking of the next bird and not concentrating on the one in hand. The dead birds may be used to swell the decoy picture; go out during a lull and set them up. If one should happen to fall on its back this will frighten the newcomers so that they will no longer come in.

At all times keep the killing area clear. If birds shy off for no apparent reason check your hide discipline, make sure your cover is not dislodged so that you are visible, that your artificial decoys are not shining in the sun—this is a notorious frightener—and that your decoy area is not a mass of loose feathers or carelessly dropped dead pigeons. Walk out into the field and take a good look: if there is anything untoward which a real pigeon might expect not to see, then change it.

It all looks very easy when written down but since it is a proper and challenging field sport, there is much to go wrong, especially nowadays when pigeons are generally suspicious of hides and decoys and have even changed their feeding habits somewhat. There was a time when every pigeon would come confidently to your decoys but now they tend to circle warily or spend long periods of prime daylight hours, not feeding as once they would but sitting in the woodland trees. When they do feed they do so spasmodically in a quick hit-and-run operation. However, there are still those times when they come in as kindly as in the easiest of the good old days. Only last month four shooters in Norfolk shot over 800 pigeons from one set-aside field of charlock in a single day. This was a record and not for beating, but the aim of fifty birds in a day is attainable by anyone on a reasonable field who knows how to shoot.

It is most important that the rough shooter's rule of not wasting anything is applied when the bag is large as well as when it is small. There is no point in shooting a large bag of pigeons of which you are unable to dispose. Make sure of your market and make the arrangements in advance. There are many game dealers these days who will take any game, pigeons included, so find out before how the system works before rather than after, when you have 150 pigeons on your hands in the hot weather and nothing to do with them.

When you get the birds home they should be laid on a cool garage floor on their backs and not left squashed together in sacks where they quickly 'sweat' and begin to smell. It is advisable to remove the crop contents by simply pulling off the whole crop and disposing of it, for decomposition often begins there, especially if the birds have been feeding on greenstuffs. Some birds you will need for your own use or to give to friends, but the bulk will go to the dealer and this is a good way of ensuring that they are used for food and that you have something coming in to defray the cost of your cartridges, although that was not the prime purpose of the exercise.

Thus a summary of what has become for some an obsessional sport, and to read more you should get a copy of my book on the subject, *Shooting Pigeons*, published by David & Charles, in which the whole business of this fascinating sport is explained in greater depth than is possible in a general book of this nature. As I have shown earlier, pigeons will, feature as a general quarry species in the rough shooter's bag, either shot as it blunders out of the hedge—but usually on the opposite side to you, so you need to bring a companion—or arrows over high in the winter sky or, the most challenging of all, intercepted as it flights over in a head-wind on the way to roost or ambushed in the wood itself on winter evenings. Good to shoot and eat, the wily woodie is surely the rough shooter's bread and butter.

4
The Duck Pond

**Great care must be taken when using the
check cord**

As well as the magic which is wildfowling, which John Richards has encapsulated so beautifully in the next chapter, it is possible to chase the same birds in other settings, notably on the rich farmland where they go to feed. The wildfowl population generally is increasing, with home-bred Canada geese, migratory grey geese and most species of duck proliferating as they are protected by the nations which host them in the breeding seasons. In the magical half-lands between the tides where they flit back and forth across the marshes they are the birds of the true wildfowler, but inland too they make a fair and challenging quarry which ought not to be sniffed at by the purist coastal fowlers.

Geese may be ambushed in the feeding grounds much as pigeons, by using decoys and finding the right field. This is a sport which tends to pall if it is overdone, for dead geese are not by law saleable and there seems to be little point in shooting great numbers of them, which sometimes can be all too easy. The shooter is taking a harvest of a wild bird and doing little or nothing to ensure its survival, but the modern concept is of responsibility and conserving and in some way protecting and preserving habitats and thus species to make sure there is something there for future generations to pursue.

The flight pond is a good example of something which can be created from very little, can be made an attractive shooting habitat and, in addition, becomes a place for many other life forms. Many authorities and organisations encourage pond-digging these days and farmers too are keen

89

in times of recession to increase the amenity value of their land by improving it. A pond is an easy way of doing this at a modest cost.

On low-lying ground with a high water table there will be no problem, just dig a hole and, as at the seaside, it will fill with water. My own little pond is a case in point; lying as it does in the washland of a fenland river, it assumes the water level of the river itself and more or less maintains it despite the state of any drought. On higher, well-drained ground you will need to insert a puddled clay lining or plastic sheet; this is to be avoided unless you have no alternative for the operation is expensive and has to be done expertly. Small streams or running ditches may be dammed but permission must be obtained from the National Rivers Authority for this, or for any other operation which involves abstraction.

Choose a site which is away from the public gaze and from footpaths, for wildfowl are shy by nature and will not care for regular disturbance by well-meaning dog-walkers. You might be caught between a cleft stick here as, if you apply for a County Council grant, one of the expectations is that the work will be visible from a public right of way. The pond needs to be handy for some sort of vehicular access for there will be times when you need to get close to the margin with tools, gear of various sorts, sacks of corn to feed the duck and, every five years or so, the heavy machinery will need to return to clean out the accumulated silt.

Mallard and teal, the dabbling duck which you are hoping to attract, cannot feed in deep water for they do not dive for their food. Therefore your pond must have good areas of shallows where you can feed and where the birds will feel welcome. There ought to be deep areas too, especially if you intend to add a few carp for interest, and to take account of the fact that a prolonged drought could have you in trouble unless you have a regular water supply and are not entirely at the mercy of the fluctuating water table. The shallows for duck ought to be not much deeper than about ten inches and the deep areas for fish could be as deep as you like but not less than about a metre and a half. All banks should be shelving with no sudden drops or submarine cliffs.

The layout should include an island, easy enough to make if you are starting from scratch for the digger simply pulls the spoil towards him, working round himself as he goes, until he retreats by a little causeway he has left for himself and which he removes behind him. An island adds character to a pond and provides a nesting-habitat for wildfowl and pheasants which is safe from all but the most determined foxes.

The banks should contain as many minor bays and miniature promontories as you can manage. This provides a great length of bank for a comparatively moderate acreage of water. The margins of any water are critical for the plant life they support, which in turn plays host to countless insects which feed young duck. Another good, general rule is to make your pond as large as you possibly can. Once the man and machine are on site it costs comparatively little more per hour to get him to enlarge your original plans. What is certain is that the moment he rumbles out of sight and onto his low-loader you will have identified at least four places which you wish you had asked him to dig out while he was about it.

THE DUCK POND

Trees are a mixed blessing. Resist the urge to rush in and jab in willow sapling round the margins, bemused by pictures of the Cambridge Backs and punts gliding between the trailing fronds. No tree should be planted closer than a minimum of fifteen metres to the edge of a pond. Trees grow, faster than you might think: in time their leaves fall in the water and pollute it; the canopy of their boughs shades water from life-giving sunlight; in time the wildfowl will be puzzled at how to land as the trees have grown so tall. Keep all tree planting well away from the edge of the pond and limit yourself to one or two small ones bang in the middle of your island.

Water plants will colonise soon enough of their own accord. I spent one year planting in my pond every water plant that kind friends donated and some I transplanted from the wild. The following decade was passed in seeking to control some and eradicate others, for weeds in a shallow, warm pond will grow so quickly that they come to cover the whole surface of the water with the exception of the deepest places.

Keep the spits and promontories weed-free by spraying with non-toxic Roundup and a garden sprayer. These open areas are essential for duck ponds as the birds like to rest there during odd moments and they do not care to be too close to thick cover where a fox might be creeping up on them. These 'Loafing Areas', as they are known, are important to the success of your pond. The Game Conservancy has produced a full-length book on the vexed question of flight pond construction and anyone seriously considering taking the matter past the drawing-board stage would be well advised to get hold of a copy.

A better, far cheaper and easier proposition is to clear out an existing pond. Local help may well be available for this and I have pressed into service Duke of Edinburgh Award Scheme youngsters, Scouts, local conservation volunteer groups and schoolchildren, many of whom are involved in some conservation project or other. The pond might well once have been a horse pond or dew-pond in the middle of a field; the further away from the buildings the better.

It is certain that three things will need to be done to a farm pond: the clearing of rubbish, the trimming or removal of trees standing and fallen, and a digging-out of accumulated silt.

Ponds were used as farm rubbish dumps and you would be surprised at what comes to light. Bicycles are nothing; old guns, bits of carts, bottles, lumps of unidentifiable iron, farm implements, even old motor vehicles will carpet the bottom. It can be quite fun removing these, dragging them out with a chain on a tractor and happily splashing about. A word of caution: stout working gloves and trainers are essential; the risk of cuts from broken glass or standing on dangerous objects is high and you must be careful. This is not work for very small children but must be carefully organised and undertaken. The rubbish you remove may be taken to the council tip; it is possible that for a worthwhile conservation project the council will take it away for you, but only by arrangement.

Overhanging trees will discourage duck from landing and should be removed or trimmed back savagely. Once the pond has been cleared it will become a habitat for many food chains as well as the duck. If properly made with the shallow areas I recommend, the pond will be used by the birds for feeding and resting on at night. We have seen that duck rest by day and feed at night, and you are after making a feeding pond as opposed to a day resting pond. The latter are all very well, but unpredictable, easily disturbed and generally less satisfactory than an evening flight pond.

Opposite:
A bad hide, but in the right place—better than vice versa

To make sure the duck come in requires more than just the creation of a habitat. They need to be persuaded and while a few will find and use it by chance, you are seeking a regular and substantial 'lead-in'. This may be achieved by various means, by far the most important of which is feeding. Corn scattered in the shallow areas will be found surprisingly quickly by the birds and they will come hurrying in in the evening for their supply, bringing their friends with them.

Feed daily if possible, failing which every other day, hence the need for the pond to be accessible for a quick dash down but in not too public a place. The birds will need a regular supply so that they know it is there waiting for them, otherwise they will go elsewhere. Scatter the corn here and there, do not pile it in a heap or empty it out of a sack all in one place. The idea is to keep the birds occupied all night working to find it, a grain here, another there, without the opportunity to gobble it all at once and look round seeking for more.

Do not over-feed, another common mistake. A plastic bucket of barley or wheat will keep a hundred mallard busy for a night if you have distributed it thinly enough. What is more, the birds will come hurrying in at last light in order to grab their share of it; feed too much so that there is more than enough for all and they delay until the safety of darkness, knowing well that there is plenty to go round. This is just what the shooter does not want; he wants the birds to come early while there is still light to shoot. Feeding is the key to flight pond success; if the owner cannot manage to do it, then it is worth finding a local or farm worker who will feed for him and also keep an eye on the place in exchange for a little shooting.

As a last resort there are automatic feeders which operate on a time clock system powered by a car battery. These may be set to spew out a measured amount of corn at a pre-set time each day so that even when you are away the pond is being fed. All you need to do is make sure the hopper is topped up and the battery changed from time to time. Such a feeder will need to stand in the water—all the more reason for having a good area of shallows and a firm bottom on which to stand the legs. If you have stocked with a few carp they will benefit from the food you scatter.

Hand feeding should be done in the evening and not in the morning. Do it too early and the pond will attract duck in the daytime. If you go to shoot and 150 mallard rise with a roar of wings from your pond they are unlikely to return at dusk as they are full already; there is the risk of turning your evening flight pond into a day resting pond and this you want to avoid. Whatever system you use, no corn ought to be dropped on the bank unless you have a good stock of pheasants which will come for it. All you do by being careless is waste your precious corn, feed moorhens and attract rats which is the last thing you want. Corn in the water can be eaten only by duck—and the carp, of course.

You need to spy on the pond at flight time, arriving before dusk on a late autumn evening and hiding in a place whence you may retreat without

Opposite:
A few decoys will help pull incoming duck to within range

disturbing the water and putting up all the birds. Count the duck in and you will discover that the numbers will increase each time you go. A full moon will break the pattern and cause the duck to come in late or not at all; such times are best avoided for shooting. When you think you have a regular and strong lead-in, you might risk a little shoot. The frequency of shooting fed flight ponds is a matter for some debate. Some say little and often, others more heavily but infrequently.

I am one of the latter school who believe that the pond is best left quiet for at least three weeks early in the season and maybe a fortnight in January between shoots. Regular shooting, even if you take only a few birds, has the same disturbance factor as a heavy shoot, so it is better to shoot it hard but less frequently. The birds take some time to recover their confidence, and to come again too soon will have them seeking less dangerous pastures. All wildfowl are chancy things, liable to be up and gone one night, navigating by the stars and landing on some Dutch polder next morning.

Natural hides may be set along the edge of the pond. Dig these into the spoil and make them semi-permanent, with pallets on edge through which the vegetation will grow. A conspicuous hide spoils the look of the place as well as being a contradiction in terms. Hides ought to face either towards the west so that the shooter may take advantage of the glow of the setting sun to see the birds, or facing down the prevailing wind so that landing duck will be coming towards him. When more than one gun shoots the pond—and most ponds ought to be able to take four or more, depending on size—it is essential to have them in a straight line all along one edge.

To have guns facing each other across the water is potentially lethal. Duck can come in very quickly and the idea of someone following a bird down and firing later than intended almost as it touches the water is too awful to contemplate. Place everyone in a straight line with clear directions as to where everyone is and all will be well. Do not allow anyone to shoot at wounded duck on the water. These are best left for the dog or for gathering next morning. Pellets ricochet off the water even when the shot was at a steep angle and can do damage; people tend to get excited in such a case and behave out of character. There is also the risk of a dog being shot, for the head of a labrador furrowing the water in the quarter light can look remarkably like a swimming mallard, especially if that is what you are looking for.

Allow the birds to come well in before shooting. Like roost shooting for pigeons, all you do at long range is wound and frighten. A hopeful 'pop-pop' at duck high in the firmament coming over for a look-see with no intention yet of landing, does no more than waste ammunition and warn the duck to choose this night to go somewhere else.

A dog is essential for almost all rough shooting and it is little short of irresponsible to go out without one. The arguments are too well rehearsed to need repeating here. It is even more important that a duck shooter has a dog available; if not his own, then that of a friend or someone who will come with him when he shoots just to pick up the birds. A duck out of reach on the pond, lying dead in thick rushes, flying on to drop over the far hedge, wounded and making its escape into the reeds, all taking place in near darkness, makes the case plain. A dog will gather such birds in a few moments, fill the bag and leave the shooter with a clear conscience. No point at all in shooting something you have no hope of ever retrieving.

Duck will come in with more confidence if you use a few decoys on the pond. Birds arriving would expect to see one or two earlier brethren down on the water and half a dozen commercial decoys will provide the reassuring blobs which cause the newcomers to drop in without hesitation. Put the decoys in the shallows whence they can be retrieved at the end; throw them boldly out into eight feet of water and ... I rest my case. Spread them so that the cords do not become entangled, and, as with all decoying, it pays to set the decoys further apart than you might think. At the end of the evening you might prefer to leave the decoys on the water and collect them next day.

There are two reasons for this; first, it will be dark when you gather them in and you might not care to risk a slip and unwanted bath in two feet of muddy water, but more importantly, it allows you to get away quickly with the minimum disturbance. It is important to leave your pond with fresh duck still coming in, thus preserving the precious lead-in. Break it and divert it elsewhere and it takes some time to get it re-established. A good shoot captain will blow his whistle when there are still duck in the air, no matter how tempted he may be to get 'just one more', and take his guns quickly and quietly away allowing duck to land undisturbed. Time spent collecting decoys adds to the disturbance time and reduces the shooting time.

A call is as useful for pond duck as it is for decoyed geese. The Olt 66, imported from America, is the best of the many on the market. You need to practise the three calls, the feeding chatter, the come-hither gentle quacking and the loud 'highball', as the American waterfowlers term it; used in conjunction with the decoys, a call can prove a deadly lure. On the other hand, there are times when it fails to work altogether and even scares off the birds; a wise shooter will come to recognise these moments and realise too that calling needs doing sparingly and that there is a deal of merit in silence!

5
The Magic of Wildfowling

John Richards

The weather forecast was right; it was dark and the north-westerly gale showed no sign of subsiding. Gusts of wind tugged at the roof-slates and intermittently showers of heavy rain battered on the windows. I sat inside the warm cottage, snugly comfortable, in my favourite armchair drawn up in front of a blazing fire. My black labrador Tor lay beside me oblivious to the world, spread-eagled, twitching occasionally as dogs do, completely relaxed and at peace with the world. I checked the tide-tables once again; a twenty-eight-foot tide high at 1.30am and a waning moon.

It was time to make a move. I rose from my chair and cautiously opened the back door, peering out into the darkness. It had been full dark for two hours but there, on the eastern horizon, was a strengthening light which I knew heralded the first signs of the rising moon. At that moment Chris, my 'fowling partner, pulled up in front of the house. He was ready for the marsh except for his waders and fortunately I also had everything ready. The list was firmly embedded in my mind, gun, cartridges, waders, cammo coat, waterproof trousers, game-bag, hat, wading stick, flask of tea. I thrust my hand into the side pocket of my jacket to check that I had my wigeon call, marsh permits, the old brass compass, the dog whistle and all the small trinkets which have a permanent place in an old coat. Within minutes

**The wildfowler and pigeon decoyer must be
an expert hide-maker**

Chris's car was loaded. Tor was suddenly wide awake and making friends with Teal in the back of the estate car. As we travelled the three miles to the marsh-side parking place, we discussed tactics and contemplated the likelihood of a successful flight. Conditions looked perfect but we concluded that wildfowlers are born optimists. Just as we parked the car it started to rain heavily. We sat talking as we waited for the shower to subside. Chris estimated that there were a thousand wigeon using the estuary and some excellent evening flights had been reported. Now, at the end of November, we knew that the birds would prefer to flight in under the cover of moonlight rather than risk running the gauntlet of guns at flight time. The rising tide would be critical; tonight it was perfect, coinciding with the moonrise which should occur soon after 8.30. We could only hope now for ideal cloud cover so as to silhouette the birds against the moon. It was a calculated gamble, one which Chris and I had taken many times before. Only another wildfowler could appreciate this marshland adventure.

The shower had now blown out as we left the car and followed the sea wall for half an hour; the pace was brisk and fortunately the rain held off. We crossed the two sluices which drain the marshland behind the sea wall. Another shower blackened the night, and we sheltered under the bank waiting for it to pass. We set off again, striking out across the marsh crossing shallow pools and gutters surrounded by spartina and sea purslane. We stopped occasionally to try and detect the faintest sound of wigeon. During the storm the moon had risen and now, quite by magic, moonbeams lit our world. Momentarily the moon could be seen clearly, seconds later thick cloud obscured the orb except for a misty impression. Another gust of wind and the clouds thinned, new moonbeams fell upon the marsh, then they were gone. It was a magical night, near perfect for flighting. Small waders moved by our intrusion could be seen clearly now as they rose, only to be carried like autumn leaves away on the wind. We stopped once more to listen. We had arrived at the outer edge of the inner marsh, where the spartina gave way to a broader expanse of sticky, glutinous mud. A place where the *Zostera* grew in abundance amongst the muddy pools and shell-bank outcrops. An exchange of words was blown away on a gust of wind. I pointed north, Chris nodded and beckoned north-east. I acknowledged his signal and shouted, 'Good luck'.

As I set off again thoughts turned to the state of the tide. It was now 9pm, four and a half hours before high water. I calculated the outer banks should be starting to cover and the first wigeon must be on the move. All I could hear were shanks and curlew, moving uneasily on their roost to the north-west. As I splashed out across the marsh more small waders flushed in front of me, then the unmistakable shapes of four wigeon jumping from the mud less than two hundred yards from where I stood. Momentarily they were silhouetted against the racing cloud cover. I made a mental note of the place where they had risen and quickly made my way to where I thought I had seen the birds. Tor had also seen them rise and as soon as we arrived she clearly sensed that the birds had been feeding on the zos.

The moon had now climbed higher and seemed much smaller, but the wind had not abated and the stiff north-westerly wind would ensure good moving cloud cover. I knew also that the birds would have to head to the wind before landing and with careful positioning the moon would enable me to see their approach. I thought of Chris: by now he must have been half a mile from me but because he had moved away downwind it would be unlikely that I would hear his shots. Suddenly a pack of wigeon tore downwind to my right; a faint 'whe...ooo' of the cock could be heard. I contemplated my position: should I move or stand my ground? Seconds later four more wigeon alighted on the mud less than thirty metres from me; their silent approach had caught me completely by surprise. A moment later the birds flared and were carried away by the wind. The chance was past. Tor wagged her tail, and I knew more birds were on the way.

To anyone who has never shot wigeon under the moon it is difficult to describe the excitement that I now felt. Seconds later the wind carried the sound of those wigeon to me. I responded, calling to the cock bird. There like the flourish of an artist's brush a pair of birds were painted against the cloud, as if they had been hanging there for an interminable time. I fired twice and Tor collected two fine birds. A cock and a hen, both in full adult plumage. Before the second bird was to hand the air was full of birds, racing past, calling, little bunches hunting the marsh before alighting. Opportunity after opportunity flashed by, three more shots without success, excitement, exhilaration, birds jinking away, others landing clearly visible on the glistening mud. It was time to revise my tactics. I needed to position myself more carefully to get a clear silhouette of the birds as they turned and made their final approach. To shoot downwind birds was hopeless and flaring

birds lifting from the mud were impossible to see. Two mallard swung in unexpectedly on my right. The drake fell to my second barrel. Tor retrieved it, followed by two more wigeon. Little packs of birds numbering seven or eight seemed totally committed to the patch where I now stood; to hesitate on a shot meant that they landed on the mud only to be flushed when the next shot was fired. I sent Tor for a wounded bird and whilst she was away shot two more wigeon, which lay motionless in a moonbeam shrine, clearly visible from the position where I crouched.

Now I detected a new sound. I could hear waves breaking on the sandbank and could see the glistening water pushing over the mud-flats. I knew that within ten minutes my position would be precarious. Wigeon were still flighting in but I had two birds to pick and it was almost time to move. The back channel flooded two and a half hours before high water and on a twenty-eight-foot tide the gutter would soon be uncrossable. Tor returned with the wounded bird. By now a thin glistening line of water had crept across the mud towards me like a silver plate on which the two dead birds were carried slowly to where I stood. Tor and I watched them, pausing to marvel at the devastatingly beautiful surroundings, then she splashed out to retrieve. There was no time to lose, and with the birds safely secured in the game-bag we turned for home, walking quickly in front of the tide and reaching the back channel as the first of the tide pushed everything before it. In half an hour it would be too deep to cross but by then we would be safely under the sea wall. The marsh once more belonged to the 'fowl, the tide had dismissed its late night visitors, the birds would now feed in peace.

In the moonlight I could make out the outline of the hawthorn bush where I knew Chris would be waiting. Sure enough he was there, huddled out of the wind with Teal beside him. It was now close to midnight and in the shelter of the sea wall we exchanged a shot-by-shot account of the wonderful flight that we had both enjoyed. Chris had heard my shots as he was downwind of my position. He knew that I had had plenty of chances to fill the game-bag. It soon became apparent that he also had had his chances, the wigeon had flighted in on a broad front and continued to hunt the marsh as the tide rose. Chris had shot well and had picked up nine wigeon. We watched the tide flood, talking and sharing a mug of tea. We laughed about the infuriating nights when we could only hear the whicker of wings and nothing could be seen against the clear moon. Then there were the nights that we came out and found that the duck had moved inland to feed as a result of changing weather conditions. There were so many tales of blank flights, but tonight we had enjoyed the flight of a lifetime.

The memories of successful forays are etched deep into the wildfowler's mind; they are unforgettable experiences, red-letter days. Yes, luck must always play an important role but a good 'fowler does not depend on good fortune alone. He will study and try to understand his quarry. So much of his sport is about the personal satisfaction of being able to understand a wild place. Success is often dependent upon spending time observing, reasoning and contemplating. And, when man seems hell-bent on his own destruction, this solitude which the wildfowler gains from his sport seems more precious than ever. I have often tried to explain this sincerity to birdwatchers who enjoy the beauty of wildfowl but have no wish to shoot them. I respect their views but I also have no hesitation in pointing out that much of wildfowl conservation and the preservation of wetland habitat that we know today was started by wildfowlers recognising there was a need for wetland conservation. They formed their own reserves and sanctuaries long before statutory controls were introduced.

It was 1841 when Colonel Peter Hawker first wrote his book *Instructions to Young Sportsmen*. Since then a remarkable number of books have been written about the sport. For students of wildfowling the array of textbooks might seem confusing. If I were to choose one, then I would recommend the third edition of *The New Wildfowler*, published by the British Association for

Shooting and Conservation, but I beg you not to pass by the works of John G. Millais, Abel Chapman and Stanley Duncan.

Books may be invaluable but, to the newcomer, they only form a basis of understanding. To experience fully the magic of wildfowling you must accompany an experienced 'fowler. I have been fortunate to spend time in the company of two great sportsmen, Arthur Cadman and the late Dr Jeffery Harrison; both taught me more in a single day in their company than I could possibly have ever learned from a book. I urge anyone going to the shore for the first time to persuade an 'old hand' to guide you. His knowledge of the marsh will fascinate you; as an ornithologist he will immediately identify birds which you will not be able to recognise. He will also make sure you come home safely! I remember being taught to cross channels where they are widest, for it is here that they are shallow. To carry a wading stick to help avoid the mudholes. To read the tide-tables accurately so as not to be left stranded on the marsh. Some lessons you will never forget. I recall walking parallel to the sea wall for three-quarters of a mile, simply because I had lost my bearings when looking for a crippled duck and had no compass. They are all mistakes which are easy to make but if at all possible they should be avoided. If such an incident occurs on your first trip, rest assured that it is likely to deter you from ever retracing your footsteps.

Many years ago, two friends visited Scotland to shoot grey geese. On arrival they employed the services of a local guide. This amicable rogue knew the ground like the back of his hand. He assured his clients that he had permission to shoot on the adjoining farmland. At daybreak the guide positioned his guns in the sand dunes at the back of the marsh, but strangely he remained below the high water mark. This puzzled the two gunners until, after several successful shots, an angry figure appeared, shouting abuse and asking what right my friends had to be on his land. They apologised profusely, assuring the laird that all would become clear when the guide returned; however, to their dismay, their guide now appeared to be a running figure almost a mile from the scene of the crime! The legalities of the sport are well documented, and I do not propose to go into them here. Do join the BASC and read their excellent Codes of Practice for the sport; I am sure they contain all the essential information that a wildfowler could wish to know.

Books are fine in theory. When it comes to understanding wildfowl there are a number of general rules which are often quoted. Most textbooks will explain that ducks will roost during the day far out on the sandbanks or on a large expanse of water, and at dusk they will flight to feed. Geese, on the other hand, roost on open water or on mud-flats during the night and flight to feed at daybreak, often on agricultural land behind the sea wall. The theory is, of course, entirely correct but, in practice, the movement of 'fowl is influenced by a number of major factors. Perhaps the most potent are the forces of the tide, the moon cycle, weather conditions and the availability of feed. Shooting pressure can also be an important factor, as too can the pattern of migration during the winter months. Successful flighting is invariably brought about by sound judgement.

For many years I travelled to the Solway with the late Ian Richardson and experienced wildfowlers from mid-Wales. We stayed at the Powfoot Golf Hotel, usually arriving for the last week of the foreshore wildfowling season around the 12 February. It was a happy event, when we always met many old friends. We arrived on a Sunday, explored the surrounding countryside and found where the geese were feeding. At night we would check the flightlines and plan our tactics for the Monday morning flight. We soon learned that the grey geese that flighted onto the marsh at dusk seldom took the same flightline to their feeding ground the following morning. The reason was quite simple. During the night the tide would lift the roosting geese from the exposed mud-flats and, according to the height of the tide, would float the army of roosting birds higher up the estuary. When the wind blew from the north the geese sheltered in one area and when a south-westerly gale blew they chose another sheltered bay. When the moon had risen before sunset, the pinks often stayed on the feed all night, but on a waning moon the birds would flight as usual at dusk then, after dark, as the moon rose, they would begin to move inland to feed under the moon. I learned also that the places I chose to shoot geese were seldom rewarding in terms of duck. In fact, to shoot duck at morning flight whilst waiting for the geese to flight on a flat calm morning made you a positively unpopular figure amongst fellow wildfowlers! These are not secrets, they represent information which is gleaned from experience and by taking the advice of others.

Consider the wildfowler who arrives two hours before evening flight and walks three miles of shoreline looking for the tell-tale signs of wigeon cheroots (droppings). His time has been well spent if he finds a place on the marsh which has been hit by the wigeon the previous night. The likelihood is that they will flight again to savour the delicacy that had previously attracted them. Contrast this 'fowler's field-craft with the man who parks his car as close to the place he wishes to flight as possible and walks to the tide edge on the off-chance of intercepting a mallard flighting from the tideline to the feeding ground. In terms of duck each may have had a rewarding flight but the man who spent his time trying to understand his marsh will, in the long term, be the better wildfowler. The crux of good wildfowling is to study and understand what is going on throughout the winter on your particular patch.

When the season starts on 1 September, good sport is gained from home-bred mallard, with the opportunity of shooting a few early migrants, perhaps wigeon and teal from Iceland or Russia and pintail from northern Scandinavia. If you are lucky enough to shoot over a goose marsh you may find that the pink-footed geese arrive during the first week of September. Their passage from Iceland comes a month before the huge flocks of greylags which also nest in Iceland. The pink-footeds will have moved to Britain early in September because their breeding grounds are located deep in the interior of Iceland. With the onset of inclement weather they are forced to move and flight early to our shores. Greylags nest on the low ground, grassy coastal

Overleaf:
The fowler is privy to sights and sounds denied to others

plains where the onset of winter is much slower; consequently they can hold their ground much longer before there is pressure to make the flight to Scotland.

With the onset of the colder weather in October and November comes the major influx of migratory 'fowl and waders. The birds take up their traditional wintering haunts. Many wigeon move south and west across the country as their northern feeding grounds become depleted. Other species have long traditions of visiting special wintering haunts. In this instance the birds make straight for these sanctuaries. Here in North Wales, on the Dee Estuary, the first pintail arrive early in September, building up in numbers throughout October and November, and remaining throughout the winter, whereas wigeon, teal and mallard numbers fluctuate according to the severity of the weather in other parts of the country. With the spring tides occurring in November and December the movement of 'fowl will alter again. Winter rains flood inland pastures and this will cause birds to move inland. Late season cold weather, snow and ice often forces birds to move from Scandinavia and Europe seeking food and shelter on our shores. At such times 'fowling on the east coast will be at its best. Birds are also driven to the coast when inland flood areas become frozen. Nowadays severe weather is monitored closely and a statutory ban on shooting can be imposed in the event of a prolonged spell of cold weather.

When the season ends on 20 February the foreshore 'fowler may experience a feeling of emptiness. His marsh becomes a peaceful sanctuary for birds congregating ready for their spring migration to the northern breeding grounds. Throughout March the days lengthen and there is a sense of uneasiness amongst the 'fowl. Suddenly, one morning they are gone, drawn by instinct to a far-off land where they can breed untroubled by human disturbance. Now the wildfowler plays a different role. Many rear ducks to release them onto unshot sanctuaries run by their clubs, others help with local conservation schemes, improving wildlife habitat. On our estuary it is the wildfowlers who are called out when, during the summer months, unsuspecting visitors fall foul of the rising tide and need to be led to safety. June and July may bring a new crop of labrador or springer puppies or a visit to the gunmaker to overhaul the trusty three-inch Magnum. Then, one evening in August, there is once again a chill in the air. The summer months have brought change, fresh saltmarsh means new feeding places for duck. Familiar landmarks are checked, sandbanks have changed and gutters may be deeper. The challenge is to try and understand this wild place again. When 1 September arrives the wildfowler will be there, if only to celebrate the beginning of another season. This is a wildfowler's year.

Many years ago my ambition was to shoot a grey goose on the shore. Year after year I went to Scotland but for one reason or another success evaded me. Then, one November morning, in the far north of Scotland, I was flighting on a remote estuary. I lay with my labrador in a shallow grave, watching the first pale streaks of dawn as they broke from the eastern skyline. It was a most unlikely place but for three mornings in succession a skein of six geese had crossed this very spot. Only now had the tide allowed me access to this place. As dawn broke I waited anxiously, straining to hear the faintest sound of geese in the bay. As it grew light, wigeon that had been feeding throughout the night came pouring over my position. I imagined the bag that I might have had if I had shot. But I did not fire, I waited and still no geese came. By now it was quite light and slowly my optimism ebbed like the tide away from me. Then a faint gaggle, a sound which I had heard so many times before. Greylags: they were there and they were about to lift. Silence now. I knew they were on their way. I hardly dared to look, pressing deeper into the grave and pushing the dog beneath me. On they came, six greylags, the same six that I had watched before, thirty feet above the sand. My grip tightened on the William Ford three-inch Magnum, now loaded with one and a half ounces of number three shot. A final glance to check their course. Dismay! I had got it wrong, they would pass a hundred metres to my right. They never deviated from the course and headed purposefully on the line that they knew so well. I walked back to the car even more determined to shoot my first greylag. The next day was my last day in Scotland. As dawn broke I waited once more for the geese that I knew would come. Success is never certain but that morning they followed the same route and I returned triumphant with a single bird from the skein of six.

I shall never forget that goose. I was fascinated by the fact that it had come all the way from Iceland to winter in Scotland. I imagined one day following the geese back to Iceland and exploring their breeding grounds. That opportunity was to come in 1987 when I, along with three wildfowling friends, retraced the late Peter Scott's adventure which he so vividly recounts in his book *A Thousand Geese*. With the assistance of an Icelandic guide, Ottar Sigurdsson, we travelled much of the Icelandic coast, visiting the lowland breeding areas of the greylag geese. A week later on the 8 July, we reached the interior, where we left our vehicle. We then crossed the Thjorsa, the largest glacial river in Iceland, and trekked into the interior where we camped in the very heart of the oasis known as Thjorsarver. Here hundreds of pink-footed geese nest every year. That was an amazing adventure which I shared with 'fowling friends and one which perhaps more than any other has made us all appreciate the magic of wildfowling.

6
The Rough Shooter's Dog

Jack Davey

**Make sure your instructions are fully
understood**

The Job to be Done

A craftsman chooses his tools very carefully according to the job to be done. Similarly, before attempting to choose a dog for the 'rough shooter' we must be quite clear in our minds what needs to be done so that we can select the right 'tool' for the job in hand. Rough shooting will have been defined elsewhere but this enquiry is only to find the most suitable dog for rough shooting.

The term 'rough shooting', like 'coarse fishing', tends to have a somewhat derogatory tone hinting at a lesser or lower form of these sports. In my younger days I don't recall the adjectives being used and shooting was shooting and fishing was fishing. Today some people refer to a day's rough shooting as a 'walked-up day', which sounds a little better than rough shoot; implying a contrast to a driven or formal day's shooting where the guns stand at a peg or stand and pheasants are driven over them by a team of beaters under the control of a keeper or keepers. Behind the guns will be the

Opposite:
A brace of springers eager to go

111

pickers-up, those very serious dog people who specialise, sometimes fanatically, in well trained, efficient retrieving machines to pick up dead and wounded game—often referred to as 'hoovering up' after the drive.

Rough shooting is an informal day with no regimented beaters and keepers to provide birds to shoot, just a solitary gun or a group of friends spending an enjoyable day in the countryside shooting a mixed bag for the pot.

Thinking more of the expression 'walked-up day'—a couple of friends ambling about the countryside are not likely to see much sport, unless game is very thick on the ground, without some sort of personal beater, (a good dog), to thrash about in cover close by to flush out hidden game. It is possible to shoot some things without a dog but it's still very impractical and limiting, especially retrieving from cover and water! I think it should be illegal to shoot without a dog present, but it is not. It is certainly immoral.

I was very fortunate to have been born and bred into real rough shooting country—a little village on the Norfolk–Suffolk borders close to the Thetford area, famous for its driven pheasant shoots. It's surprising how far pheasants stray. Close on fifty years ago my science master implanted in my mind that nature abhors a vacuum, which is not only a fact of science but also very true of wildlife. As we removed the odd pheasant from our land, creating a vacuum, so it was replaced. Our area had a constant supply of pheasants to enhance the bag.

Our village was ideal terrain for providing mixed shooting, ranging from arable land and woods to marshes and reedbeds by the river, providing a good mixed habitat for rabbit, pigeon, partridge, pheasant, duck and sometimes snipe and woodcock. My introduction to shooting was during the war years when game, pigeon and rabbits were very much sought after to help out the meagre food ration. As a schoolboy a few rabbits or pigeons and the odd duck or pheasant were a lucrative means of providing pocket money for the school tuck-shop. During the winter months I was as well off as anyone in our form.

I wasn't a 'natural' and my success with the gun didn't come easily or quickly. Without the enthusiastic help of Gyp, a cross-bred terrier, I would have returned home many a time empty-handed. My friends in the village and I all had these rather long-legged black and tan mongrel terriers—real 'Heinz 57s' they were but, nevertheless, first-class ratters and rabbiters, providing they were allowed to do it their way. They hunted rabbits and pheasants furiously and noisily, in fact they chased everything that moved and gave tongue whilst in pursuit or on a hot scent. Often it was necessary to sprint fifty metres to keep within gunshot of the dog in case anything was flushed from cover. If a rabbit was pushed out of a form more than fifty metres from cover or burrow it would be lucky to escape being caught. When we hunted a little pack of these dogs they seem to mesmerise rabbits. I think it was because they swarmed all over the place and a rabbit didn't know which way to turn to escape.

Incidentally, should you ever need a long-legged, black and tan 'Heinz 57' terrier then I will let you into the secret of picking a good pup out of a litter— it must have four eyes, which means a tan spot about the size of a sixpence (sorry: present-day, five pence piece) just above each eye, and the roof of its mouth must be mottled black and pink.

There were a few pedigree dogs about the village. I can recall one farmer with a black labrador retriever and another with a spaniel. Most of the dogs used for shooting were cross-bred gun-dogs or terriers, often with some collie in them.

It was said that pedigree dogs were useless for our type of shooting—no nose and no stamina—and were something for the upper classes to use on driven pheasant shoots where the dogs didn't have to work, only pick up shot pheasants falling onto open ground. Stamina was not a word to be found in the Norfolk vocabulary at that time and what was more likely to have been heard about pedigree dogs in the vernacular was 'them owd thurrer-bred dawgs aint no good they git knocked up tew qwikly'. I think it was really just an excuse for only being able to afford a few shillings for a dog instead of a few pounds. As a schoolboy my first two terriers were 'free to a good home' dogs but in the early fifties, when in my early twenties, I paid the financially crippling sum of fifteen shillings (75p) for a cross-breed.

The Dog for the Job

Today, the majority of shooting people understand and appreciate the value of careful and selective dog breeding. Pedigree gun dogs are sought after, not only for use on the formal driven pheasant shoot, but also for work on rough shoots, where it is really important, if the dog is to be an asset, that it is well trained and obedient. So many times I have been asked to provide a dog and the prospective purchaser has pointed out 'not one of your best dogs, a

partly trained one will do, as I only want it for rough shooting'. I'm sure the word 'rough' is the trouble as it suggests something not quite up to standard—we often talk disparagingly of 'roughnecks', 'rough diamonds' and 'rough customers'—so 'rough shoot' and 'rough dog'. This is just not so. I contend that it is just as important, if not more so, to have a good, well disciplined dog on a rough shoot as on a driven shoot.

If a dog misbehaves on a driven shoot it can be pegged down during the drives and just allowed to pick up afterwards, thus not spoiling the day's shooting. On a rough shoot, a wild unruly dog not only ruins the day's shooting but also ruins friendships. If it is put on the lead it then becomes worse than useless.

If a day's rough shooting is to be enjoyable and successful a dog is

Opposite:
Black labrador: one of the most popular all-rounders

necessary to provide the sport, to act as a personal beater and then to pick up afterwards. It must always hunt within range of the gun, be steady to flush shot and fall, retrieving only on command. It must be an enthusiastic hunter with speed and style, and fearless in all types of cover. It needs to be an accurate marker and a positive retriever from cover and water, with a soft mouth. A good nose is essential to find game, both unshot and shot, in dense cover, especially to find wounded game and quickly return it to hand for humane despatch. It must be free of all vices such as whining, yapping, chasing and hard mouth. A good biddable temperament is essential, with no aggression towards people or dogs. A tall order, you may think—not really, because selective breeding of pedigree gun dogs has produced strains of dogs with many of the qualities needed genetically fixed or dominant, and many of the bad traits bred out. All that is needed is good training and handling.

Looking back to that Norfolk village of my youth with its variety of cover ranging through woods and scrubland, overgrown hedgerows of bramble and thorn, fields of sugar-beet and kale, rushy marshes and huge reedbeds by the river: I realise now that my wonderful, highly prized, much loved cross-bred black and tan terriers were not really the ideal dogs for the job. Their coats were not thick enough for the really tough cover, they gave tongue, chased everything that moved and flushed most things out of range. They would only tackle cover with drive and determination if they chased a rabbit into it or if they picked up scent from the outside, but hunting *for* scent, as opposed to being *on* scent in tough cover was not a strong point. Stinging nettles were avoided unless scent oozed from them to encourage entry, and retrieving from water was often a failure. Generally they pleased themselves about where they went and what they did and you had to follow. Terriers are renowned for being difficult to train, being hard-headed and with a will of their own. This must be expected, as a terrier's real job is going to ground to face foxes and badgers, when a hard aggressive temperament *is* called for which doesn't lend itself to easy training and biddability.

Now that I have fifty years of dogging experience behind me, covering the cross-bred terriers, various spaniels and retrievers, and also forty-six years of rough shooting experience, I am quite sure I know the dog that suits me and my type of shooting. Just to keep you in suspense a little longer and to show that I am not biased, I will look at the various gun dog groups and how they lend themselves to rough shooting.

The Pointers and Setters

I must be honest and admit that I have little experience of the bird dogs, in fact I should say no experience at all. I have never considered them as serious contenders for the position of a rough shooter's dog. I have not lived or shot in a countryside that called for the very specialised work of a pointer or setter, as the whole of my life has been spent in the eastern counties and in the West Country. The shooting in these areas does not call for the services of these breeds.

If your rough shoot happens to be on a wild windswept Yorkshire or Scottish moor then a pointer or setter could well be the dog for you, especially if the quarry density averages a covey of grouse to 500 acres of heather-clad hillside. A close-hunting spaniel would take all day to make a find, but a good pointer or setter with its long legs galloping over the heather, quartering a wide pattern of some 150 yards each side of its handler, would make a find in a reasonably short time. One snag could be that if you shoot your grouse you will need another dog of the retrieving breeds to pick it up, because your bird dog doesn't often retrieve.

The Retrievers

The retrievers most commonly seen in the shooting field today are the Labrador, the Golden, the Flat-coated and, very occasionally, the Curly-coated and the Chesapeake Bay. They are all equally good but, without any doubt, the Labrador Retriever is by far the most popular.

Retrievers, particularly the Labrador, increased dramatically in numbers following the development of the breech-loading shotgun and the move towards *battue* or driven bird shooting, with the employment of gamekeepers and the hand-rearing of large numbers of pheasants. Consequently large bags of driven pheasants were shot and dogs were no longer needed to hunt up and flush birds to shoot, as previously, but to act as straight retrievers either to sit sedately beside a gun at a peg or behind the line with a handler, to pick up large numbers of shot birds after the drive. This specialised work called for a big, strong dog that was a fast and efficient retriever. The retrievers, as the name suggests, are purely for retrieving and for generations have been selectively bred entirely for that purpose, and hunting thick rough cover is not a strong point.

Some people do use them as a hunting dog to flush unshot game for the gun. This may be possible on a walked-up day in roots and similar light cover but would not be very successful in dense punishing cover such as bramble, thorn and gorse. They are good for pigeon shooting and duck shooting, and in particular wildfowling, because they like water, being very strong swimmers with good water-resistant coats.

The Hunt, Point and Retrieve Group

This group is commonly referred to as the HPRs and embraces several breeds all imported from continental Europe. They are often referred to with some disdain as 'foreigners'. In the British Isles, hunt, point and retrieve dogs have not been developed. Perhaps this is because the English and also the Scots tend to favour specialisation and are not too happy with the 'Jack of all trades' situation.

In the British Isles the most common HPRs in the shooting field are the German Shorthaired Pointer, the German Wirehaired Pointer, the Weimaraner and the Hungarian Vizsla. Less commonly used here are the Münsterlander, the Brittany Spaniel and the Spinone from Italy.

Their job is a combination of the work of the pointers and the spaniels. They quarter large areas of land, come on point, flush when required and retrieve on command—what more could you want? Some people, a minority I must admit, are convinced of the utilitarian value of these dogs, and consider them the complete all-round gun dog and therefore the ideal choice for the rough shooter.

Opposite:
**Golden retriever, a good companion and
reliable fetcher and carrier of game**

I've not trained or worked any of these breeds myself so I find it difficult to judge their value as gun dogs, and where I shoot and pick up I very rarely see them. Over the years I've seen a few at work but unfortunately, I must admit, I haven't been impressed. I didn't find them exciting to watch, as they run rather plainly and their work in cover and water is unimpressive. Perhaps I had been unlucky to meet up with the wrong dogs, or on their bad days.

A lively litter of Springers: take your pick!

The Spaniels

The breeds of spaniel are numerous but most of them have dropped out of the shooting scene over the past seventy years or so. The English Springer Spaniel is the only serious working spaniel left, other than a few strains of working Cocker Spaniel still to be found doing a useful job in the shooting field. Only occasionally, indeed very rarely, do we come across a Welsh Springer Spaniel, Clumber Spaniel, Sussex or Field Spaniel at work. The minor breeds, as they are often called, have an occasional field trial to try and encourage their owners to work them, otherwise these breeds will slip into oblivion and become working gun dog history.

The English Springer Spaniel is a very popular working gun dog and many consider it as 'the maid of all work' and the rough shooter's ideal dog.

Summer pigeon hide

Top:
The results of an afternoon with the pigeons

Above:
The springer spaniel is a popular rough shooter's dog

Right:
Decoys should be set not too close together

122

Summer hedgerow stalking for pigeons

It is primarily a hunting dog and is renowned for its bramble-bashing ability. A good Springer has an insatiable appetite for cover and will tackle it with enthusiasm, hunting it for scent and not just on scent. Bracken, bramble, thorn, gorse, reeds and rushes are all on the spaniel's itinerary.

A well-trained spaniel hunts its ground in front of the gun, always quartering within gunshot. It should flush winged game and ground game, drop to the flush or the shot, remain steady and only retrieve on command. Springer Spaniels can be used, if needs be, as straight retrievers, for pigeon shooting and duck shooting.

Take Your Pick

We tend to be like our dogs. How many times has it been said: 'Like dog— like master'? Dogs are often seen as an extension of the owner's personality. This may be by conscious choice or quite by accident. Dogs are sometimes selected as a status symbol or to suit the family, the home or the car. But all these are wrong as the choice should be related to the type of shooting, the cover and conditions on the ground. The home, car or role as a status symbol are all secondary considerations, otherwise you could well finish up with a pointer to deal with woodland with impenetrable waist-high brambles or a Cocker Spaniel to tackle 1,000 acres of knee-high heather.

I think the decision is easy and can be made by the process of deduction. Those untrainable and yapping, quarrelsome, disobedient terriers of my youth are not to be considered. The pointers and setters are the first to be excluded as they are far too specialist, being geared entirely to huge expanses of open moorland. The next to go are the retrievers, as they are predominantly straight retrievers of shot game. They have been bred for generations for their trainability, docility and keen noses, and not for hunting thick cover. A retriever would be of little use on a rough shoot with a lot of punishing cover. I don't see them as all-rounders and certainly not as a dog for the rough shooter.

The choice has narrowed to HPRs and the spaniels. I must be frank and tell you that I'm not an HPR man, as you may well have gathered already. Although they have the extra attribute of pointing they fall very short when it comes to hunting cover and working in water. In my opinion they are all very much of a muchness as far as work in the field is concerned, and I would put them as the second choice for the rough shooter.

Returning to the 'like dog—like master' syndrome, the continental breeds tend to have the character and temperament of their Euromasters. According to your similarity to the German, or perhaps, French or Italian temperament you could choose your dog!

For me there is only one dog for the rough shooter and that is a spaniel, preferably an English Springer Spaniel. Secretly I like to think I have a spaniel character, with a spaniel's attitude and enthusiasm towards work, play and life in general—let's have fun and everybody is my friend. A good spaniel will tackle anything with gay abandon, even the impossible. It is the eternal optimist, expecting to find something to root out from every clump of

The Springer Spaniel is the ideal rough-shooting dog

brambles, however small, even two fronds of bracken have to be investigated, just in case.

The Commando of the Shooting Field

Because the spaniels have unlimited drive, determination and courage in cover they are often referred to as the 'Commando of the shooting field'. They make a shooting day all the more enjoyable because they put their heart and soul into it. They please you by their constant enthusiasm and their willingness to work under the most adverse conditions. They will keep you on your toes as you can never be sure what will happen next. Their tails will indicate that something is in the wind, so don't relax your concentration and be prepared for the action when it comes.

You see much more of a spaniel's tail because its head is always delving into cover. The only time you are likely to see its face, other than lunch-time, is after it delivers a cock pheasant to hand, with a twinkle in its eye that seems to say, 'How's that for a quick retrieve—you did say fetch it?'

I will let you into one or two secrets about spaniels. They are fun to have about the place—they make good family pets and can dig the garden and water it! They are happy to accept their lot and are not aggressive towards other dogs or humans. Postmen, policemen and milkmen can usually go about their legitimate business unmolested. They provide the sport which allows you to fill the bag. You can fantasise about you and your spaniel as a great team, a wild, primitive hunting-pack out to find food, each completely dependent on the other for success. One tip—you must become the pack leader and maintain that position, otherwise you will end up no better than I was with those terriers of my past.

What and Where?

Whatever breed of gun dog you choose, ultimate success means getting a well bred dog of working strain which has been thoroughly trained, followed by good management and discipline in the shooting field. The first decision is whether to buy a puppy and train it yourself, send it to a trainer or buy a fully trained dog. Beware of partly trained dogs as there is usually a good reason for parting with a 'promising' young dog. The first option means lots of know-how and patience and the others lots of money. I can tell how to get knowledge but not how to acquire patience—or, for that matter, money. If you decide to train your dog then the knowledge can be gleaned from a wealth of books and video cassettes on training gun dogs. Also there are masses of gun dog clubs and societies whose members are very willing to help and advise. Most clubs run training classes to help people to help themselves.

If you decide to send your young dog for training, make sure you take advice on where it should go. Impress on the trainer that you need it fully trained to the highest possible standard with the emphasis on discipline. Don't suggest 'it's only for rough shooting'.

If you elect to go for a trained dog then choose a reputable trainer, well known for producing good dogs. Ask among your shooting friends, or again the local gun dog club is a good source of recommendation. Be sure to exclude any dogs with show strains in them—show dogs have been bred for generations for beauty, ignoring working capabilities.

Training Your Dog

If you decide to train your dog yourself then I suggest that you take your puppy home when it is no older than seven weeks. This is the best time to split up a litter because the pups still have a 'mother image' and have not started to form a 'pack image' with litter mates. A puppy will settle down in its new environment much more readily at this age, transferring the 'mother image' to you, which at a later date you can change to a 'pack leader image'. This bonding is very important and for the first few days or weeks, if possible, the person to become the pack leader should spend as much time

as possible with the puppy. Read books on gun dog training and select from them the training methods and hints on training that suit you and your dog. Join a gun dog club and attend training classes. Be a good listener and learn from watching others. Aim for the highest level. Don't start off by telling yourself and others 'it's only for rough shooting'.

Do not be in a hurry: training a dog is a slow process, building up a little at a time on what has already been learned. Remember that a dog is only a simple animal and lives in the present, not in the past or the future. It learns from imitation, repetition, trial and error. It has limited brainpower and responds mainly to impulse and instinct. It cannot indulge, as you can, in reasoned thought. Always bring your intelligence down to the dog's level and do not expect the dog to come up to yours. You must become dominant over the dog by becoming its pack leader, always maintaining that position. Once your position is established and accepted by the dog (more readily accepted by bitches than dogs, as dogs constantly try to become pack leader by right), training and working the dog will be easier. Never relax as the dog will take an advantage.

Success

The success of any pack or social group of hunting animals depends on the pack leader. Similarly the success of your pack, albeit only a pack of two, depends on you. Keep the position you have established, which has been accepted by the dog, and you will be much more effective than any wild pack

Opposite:
Example of good teamwork, with a whiff of canine rivalry

because you have those extra ingredients, brains and the capability of reasoned thought, which makes the team really efficient. I hope you will have many successful and happy days shooting with your dog. Days that will fill you with pride and satisfaction, especially if you chose the breeding, picked the pup and finally trained it yourself. There will be disappointments, of course. I have never had a dog, however good, that didn't screw it up at some time or other—after all, they are only dogs!

I've had my embarrassing moments, but nevertheless many proud moments, lots of success, excitement and reward. Above all I've had lots of fun. I hope you do; in fact, I'm sure you will.

7
Straight Powder

Graham Downing

The end of a trying day

There are very few cast-iron rules about rough shooting; that is one of its great glories. When you are out amongst the fields and hedgerows, beating the boundaries in search of a pheasant, or perhaps down on the marsh to look for a duck, it is of no consequence what you are wearing, nor whether your gun is the product of a top London maker or an old, beaten-up semi-auto. There are no gamekeepers to tip or fixed shooting positions from which you wander at your peril. And if your dog runs in, then the chances are that nobody is going to hold it against you.

In fact there is nothing much by way of cardinal sin that qualifies you for instant dismissal from the rough shooting field. Whether the end of the day sees you with nothing to show for your empty cartridge belt or a broad grin and a bulging game-bag is immaterial: there is no requirement to shoot straight, provided always that you shoot safely.

Whether shooting alone or in company, the rough shooter, like everyone else who carries a gun, needs to be safety-conscious. Indeed, safe gun handling is perhaps something about which rough shooters need to think even harder than those who shoot driven game. At least the participant in a formal driven day has the opportunity, at the beginning of each drive, to spend a little time thinking about where and when he can take his shots. Safety zones with respect to beaters and neighbouring guns are simple to determine, and because the driven shooter will invariably be obliged to return his gun to its slip between drives, the chances of an accident occurring whilst crossing fences or gates is substantially reduced. And if the host or

Safe passing of a gun over a natural hazard

keeper on a big driven day is the slightest bit concerned about a gun's lack of experience, they will probably detail what is euphemistically called a 'loader' to stand with him and diplomatically keep an eye on the proceedings.

However, it is just those split-second decisions as to where a gun may safely be pointed and discharged which must become second nature to the rough shooter. And there are no formal rules to guide him; his grasp of gun safety must be instinctive.

Perhaps the most important safety maxim whilst out rough shooting is always to be aware, as far as possible, of where other guns are in relation to yourself. It seems simple and obvious, and perhaps, when walking up a field of sugar-beet, the location of every other member of the team is plain to see. But walk through a tall crop of maize, or, even worse, a hairy old fen with reed stems and willow-herb about your head and thick undergrowth to plough through, and it is all too easy to become disorientated and to lose contact with the gun next door.

As an old wild cock pheasant bursts out of the clinging vegetation in front of you, just allowing time for a snap shot as it disappears behind a screen of waving reed-heads, it is essential for you to know where your neighbours are. So always keep in line abreast when walking up through thick cover. If it is hard for the guns to see each other then do not be afraid to use your voice to keep in touch, and if it is particularly tough going for one member of the team, then slow down to accommodate him. Don't force the pace, because that is how accidents happen. It's not much fun when you are struggling through some particularly intractable piece of jungle, to see the rest of the line sauntering blithely on, twenty metres ahead. Even if a bird did get up in front of you, it is unlikely that either you or your colleagues would be able to shoot at it in safety.

As for carrying a gun through thick cover, that is always a difficult one. Bear in mind that the chance of a shot might present itself at any moment, and that a state of readiness is called for. But remember also that twigs and branches can easily catch in triggers and dislodge safety-catches. Just as easily can nasty little bits of vegetation get into your gun barrels. If in doubt, then check them before shooting and so avoid the risk of damage to your gun or yourself.

A particular danger arises when, on a rough shoot, you and your fellow guns split into two groups and take it in turns to stand and to walk. Ultimately there will come a time, perhaps on a beat which is unfamiliar to you, when, as a walking gun, you will approach the line of standing guns. Be ultra-careful, for it is all too easy to take a shot in front without realising that you are endangering a fellow shooter who remains obscured behind bushes or undergrowth. He will probably be waiting quietly and inconspicuously in order not to spook any game moving forward, and it is up to you to ascertain just exactly where he and the other standing guns are situated.

It is not just your fellow guns who are at risk. Any good rough shoot depends upon its dogs; not the stately sort which sit at pegs, but the workers which root out game from deep within bramble bushes and which plunge fearlessly into the thickest, most compacted cover. It is in such circumstances that dogs are sometimes put in danger by a low shot into cover. If you believe there to be a dog immediately behind that bird which has just got airborne, then it is wise to let it get well clear of the surrounding undergrowth before you fire.

I will never forget seeing a lovely yellow labrador called Mandy put a cock pheasant out of a wild patch of Norfolk marsh many years ago, shortly after I started shooting. She was an eager and willing bitch, and an absolute demon on marsh pheasants, but occasionally Mandy was a mite over-enthusiastic, and as this particular bird emerged through the top of the waving stems of willow-herb, she jumped, making a last grab for the departing pheasant's tail feathers. At the same split second the gun next to me fired, and the poor dog received the best part of an ounce of number six shot straight into her head and forequarters from about thirty-five metres. The sound of her screaming and yelping was quite pitiful, but she was rushed to the vet's surgery and, thankfully, survived the encounter. Needless to say, the day was ruined for all concerned.

Almost invariably there will be obstacles to cross on a day's rough shooting. Whether it be a barbed wire fence, a stile or a slippery ligger across a dyke, it is while negotiating an obstruction that an accident is most likely to occur. So it is simply not good enough to rely on the safety-catch as you clamber over, under or through, nor is it acceptable to break the gun, leaving the cartridges in the chambers. Always unload, and if possible pass the gun to someone else whilst climbing or crossing.

When in company, the habit comes naturally to most of us, but when alone, it is quite easy to get into the way of taking short cuts. That is how accidents happen. I find it a valuable reminder to myself, as I take my young son out shooting, to explain at each step the essential rules of safety: how to carry a gun, when to load it, where to point it and how to cross a fence with it. Such rules are the fundamentals of shooting and cannot be drummed home too often.

Rough shooting is a sport of enormous variety, and much of that variety and interest lies in the multitude of different shots which are to be encountered during a day in the field. One moment it may be the pigeon screaming high along the edge of a woodland or flashing across the top of a ride, the next it may be a rabbit jinking through the brambles or a woodcock zigzagging between the trees in front of you. However, much of the rough shooter's sport is the result of walking up crops, woodland, pasture or, preferably, wild and natural cover. Because of this, it is the going-away shot which he will most often have to deal with.

Going-away pheasants are sometimes dismissed or sneered at by the driven shooter, but that doesn't mean a going-away pheasant is an easy mark; far from it. There are a few basic points to consider before tackling such a shot, and firstly let us look at range. Sometimes, especially on a poor scenting day, when the ground cover is especially thick or when there is a

crust of snow over the ground that you and your dogs are working, pheasants will sit tight, only getting up as you are just about to tread on them. Bearing in mind the fact that everything the rough shooter kills is destined either for his own table or that of one of his friends, there is no point whatsoever in turning a pheasant into airborne pâté the moment it leaves the ground. Give the tight-sitting pheasant a bit of law before pulling the trigger, ideally taking it at a range of twenty-five metres or so. Then, if by any chance you should miss with the first barrel, there will still be time to fire the second.

Another point about pausing for a few moments before shooting at a close-sitting pheasant is that it enables you to relax and collect yourself after the momentary surprise of the bird's possibly quite unexpected emergence. A relaxed, controlled shot is far more likely to find its target than a hurried, flustered one.

The opposite pertains when shooting on one of those days when the pheasants all seem to want to run on ahead and get up forty metres in front. Then you have to be quick, and take the shot the instant it presents itself, otherwise it is out of range within a few moments. I have shot with a number of people who, armed with fully choked wildfowling guns, can knock down a fleeing pheasant at the most remarkable ranges; but that is not something to be encouraged amongst lesser shots. Too often it results in pricked or wounded birds, and it is dead pheasant in the bag which the rough shooter is after, not injured ones left at large in the countryside.

Bear in mind the question of height when dealing with the going-away shot. If there is a belt of trees or a tall hedge ahead, then a pheasant can be climbing very sharply, and it is essential to get well above it with the muzzles before firing as, nine times out of ten, such birds are missed underneath. If, on the other hand, the pheasant is a low flyer, then look carefully and make sure it is a safe shot before firing. It is not necessary always to leave a low bird, as a driven shooter would, for the objective of all rough shooting is game for the pot. Nevertheless, it is only the pheasant which the cook is interested in, not the local farm livestock or bits of agricultural machinery which may be standing by.

Next, ground game. The rabbit has been the mainstay of many a rough shooter, and I am delighted that the bunny is making such a comeback from the ghastly plague of myxomatosis. Nobody with a degree of humanity about them can truly believe that it is right for an animal to die such a horrible and lingering death as that of the myxy rabbit, even a vegetable grower such as myself. I would much prefer to see the rabbit survive to provide a ready source of excellent food and the sport which goes with it, than be exterminated by the deliberate spreading of disease.

When shooting rabbits you may well find that you are firing at a target which is seen only as it darts between clumps of grass or cover. Under these circumstances there is an almost irresistible urge to check your swing at the point where the rabbit last disappeared. Do so and you will most assuredly miss behind. Keep the muzzles moving fast, and put your shot ahead of the rabbit's nose, even if it is about to vanish from view. Many is the occasion upon which, having fired at and then lost sight of a rabbit, I have looked behind the bramble bush towards which it was heading to find the bunny stone-dead.

One of the most enjoyable opportunities for rabbit shooting is that provided whilst following the combine at harvest time. Traditionally the guns waited until the field was almost cut, and then stood around the last block of corn, waiting for the rabbits to bolt from it. That was when cereal crops were dirtier and more weed-infested than they are now. A well kept modern cornfield has little weed growth in the middle, and so not much on which the rabbits can feed. The best shooting nowadays is often around the headlands, in particular where these have been managed specially for game and treated only with a bare minimum of herbicides.

Always be careful, however, when shooting ground game. In this, more than in almost any other situation in the shooting field, it is possible to let enthusiasm lead to accidents, especially when rabbits are turning back and dodging between a line of guns. Hares can also prompt an outbreak of dangerous shooting, especially when they are pursued by unruly dogs. Unlike a rabbit, which is fairly easy to bowl over, a hare is a large animal which takes a deal of stopping. Hares should never be tackled at long range, for the inevitable result will be wounded game. If you are deliberately setting out to shoot hares, then it is best to move up a couple of shot sizes to number four. Whilst I enjoy eating hare, and am happy to shoot one when a straightforward and easily killable chance presents itself, on the whole I prefer to leave the hares for the local beagles.

One of the joys of the rough shoot is its variety. On even the tiniest piece of ground one can find a range of different habitats, and with them a whole host of quarry species. The shoot which still remains closest to my heart extends over no more than thirty acres, and yet it has everything. A rambling, old-fashioned farm on the edge of Norfolk's broadland, the land slopes down to the valley floor in a patchwork of spinneys and old pasture, linked together by thick, overgrown hedges from which you can expect to flush anything from a pigeon to a woodcock.

In what I call the Dell, an old marl working now overgrown with sycamore, sweet chestnut and holly, I have often flighted pigeons during the afternoon as they finish feeding on the high arable farmland and make their way to roost in the tall beeches of an ancient manor house on the far side of the river. Picking a small clearing with a sufficiently large 'skylight' across which the birds will flight, I keep absolutely still and wait, suitably camouflaged in the undergrowth. Again, the trick is to keep swinging on the passing pigeon as though the tracery of branches was not there. You may from time to time bring down a spattering of falling twigs, but amazingly, sufficient shot seems to get through to do the business, and if you keep at it, then the pigeons should start falling too. Personally, I must admit to a great liking for pigeon flighting. It is by no means easy shooting, and yet on an afternoon when the pigeons are moving in large numbers, it can yield some really fast sport.

But the greatest joy of the particular shoot I have described is the reedy, tangled, wilderness of a marsh and the deep, slow river which meanders past it. On a winter's afternoon the wild pheasants—'gravy stinkers' as we used to call them—draw onto the marsh to roost, encouraged by generous bucketfuls of tail barley. And as the light fades, the mallard and teal flight along the river.

To me, wildfowl are one of the highlights of a rough shoot. They provide the most exciting sport, heightened by the fact that they move during those few minutes of dawn and dusk when the light is dim, the air is electric with expectation and the senses are working overtime.

The high, overhead flighting mallard should present few problems, except for the fact that it can be difficult to judge range and speed accurately in the half-light. Suffice it to say that most mallard are missed behind. The dropping bird, planing down with paddles set in the forward position like airbrakes, is a different matter. In essence it is an easy shot to take, provided that you remember to 'float' the bird over the top of your muzzles as you track it downwards, and keep floating it until the moment you pull the trigger. The sighting picture, once learned, is unforgettable. However, should you by chance blot out the descending duck with your barrels, then you can be sure that it will be missed as it drops below the shot pattern.

Teal, zipping past in the gloaming, are targets as challenging as the finest driven partridge. They demand great concentration, quick reactions and preferably good hearing, for it is the rushing sound of their wing-beats and the low 'treep', giving that split-second warning of their imminent arrival, which can make all the difference between a missed opportunity and a shot successfully taken.

While my broadland riverbank is graced with cover sufficiently dense to conceal the waiting shooter from the eyes of wary wildfowl, on many shoots it is normal to shoot duck from a hide. This presents a new range of techniques to master. Depending upon the height of the hide, one can either shoot kneeling, sitting or standing. The first of these is perhaps more properly associated with the sort of portable hide that is used out wildfowling, and the second with pigeon decoying. It is well worth learning how to shoot from a sitting position, even in a well built, semi-permanent hide, for it saves having to stand up and adjust your footing in those precious few moments which elapse between sighting the quarry and shooting at it.

Hide discipline is important. Keep your shooting area tidy and uncluttered: remember that you may have to turn round quickly in order to deal with a bird coming from behind, and you will not wish to fall over game-bags, spare clothing or thermos flasks. As for dogs, well, some can mark the line and length of a falling bird quite well enough by sound, without actually watching it hit the deck, and they are better off in the hide with you, where they cannot be seen by approaching wildfowl. Otherwise, sit the dog immediately outside the hide, but camouflage its eyrie with a few twigs or reed stems stuck in the ground, just sufficient to break up the dog's outline. Some people claim to be able to throw a camouflaged sack over a sitting dog, but I have yet to meet an animal which is prepared to put up with such treatment without shaking off the unwanted garment.

A dog, camouflaged or not, is the rough shooter's essential companion. Not only is he or she a friend without whom you would not see more than a fraction of the game available to you on the shoot, but a dog is also essential when it comes to retrieving shot game. By this I do not mean those stone-dead pheasants which drop thirty yards out on a nice, open stubble field. It is hardly necessary to use a dog in order to pick such birds as these.

The retrieves for which you need a dog are the difficult ones, and in particular those where wounded game is involved. None of us likes to wound birds or beasts: our objective is always the clean kill. If we shoot, then sooner or later we have to come to terms with the fact that animals are not always killed outright. Under these circumstances it is absolutely imperative that every effort is made to bring the quarry to hand.

This was a lesson which was drummed into me from an early age. When, as a lad, I brought down a bird or beast, then my father insisted that it was brought to hand before we continued shooting. Sometimes a fallen pheasant, lodged deep into the willow-herb jungle for which our small shoot was notorious, would take half an hour or more to find, but very rarely did we lose one. And when we did so, then it was a cause for genuine regret and sadness. We shot for sport, it is true, but we also shot for the pot, and to kill a bird and then waste it seemed utterly pointless. It still does.

Retrieving ducks could be an even more exacting business. At one time, before we had a dog, it was my job to swim the river for any wildfowl which had been brought down on the far bank. It was a chilly operation to say the least, and not one which I particularly relished, especially after morning flight on a school day, but it certainly gave me a sense of the value in which a hunter should hold his quarry. It taught me respect for the creatures which I pursued.

That respect is something which is central to all true hunters, for without respect for your quarry, shooting becomes merely an exercise in killing, an act divorced and distanced from the natural cycle of which country sports are a part. Rough shooting is a central element of that cycle, for whilst the rough shooter takes, he takes with understanding and reverence. He also gives, in the few pheasants or partridges which he releases, the nests which he protects, and above all in the wild places which he cherishes, looks after and preserves.

8
Getting Clobbered

Time was when it did not matter. The shooter took to the field in whatever he happened to be standing up in, and very impractical much of it must have been. The stove-pipe hat of the early Victorians must have blown over the shooter's eyes at the most awkward moments every time there was a gust. The thin patent-leather boots would have been useless in the mud, and the invention of the waterproof wellington boot lay many years in the future. The original ones were made of leather (as were thigh water boots worn by fishermen and wildfowlers) and needed hours of cleaning, drying and oiling, and still they leaked. The frock coat featured in the old George Morland prints, together with the powdered wigs, all spoke of a complete lack of practicality.

In 1820 or so, the redoubtable John Mytton went duck shooting in the snow at night in his night-shirt, sometimes naked save for a night-cap, and crept over the ice in bare feet. At the merest whim he would leave the dining-room by the shortest route, through the window, and set off across country with his muzzle-loader, wearing silk waistcoat, cotton shirt and embroidered tailcoat, the ensemble topped off with silk hose and Spanish leather dancing slippers. Thus attired he would stalk the snowy wastes with no care for his personal comfort as long as there was an outside chance of getting a shot. Apart from the fact that sad man, 'Mad Jack' was both an alcoholic and totally deranged, he could well have been the patron saint of rough shooters. As things turned out, they would probably have preferred someone rather more respectable, although for my money he sounds well enough.

Nowadays we take a little more trouble to cosset ourselves. We have discovered that it is not unpleasant to be warm and comfortable and we reflect with pity mixed with envy on the fortitude of whole generations of sportsmen who would have known the pleasures of neither.

To start with the hardware: the essential element, the gun, of course, to set forth without which is to place yourself at a severe disadvantage. The short answer here is that any old fowling-piece or game-gun will do as long as it is safe. Walked-up or decoyed game need not be that hard to hit (although my colleague Graham Downing might disagree), and if you follow my advice to place yourself as close to the target *in the first stages* as you possibly can, comparatively few demands will be made on your gun. However, there are minor guidelines and points to ponder.

If Pater has bequeathed to you a pair of 'best' London side-locks, or even second-best ones, you need to decide whether the life of a hedgerow-poking, plodding, bag-filling sort of fellow is what their maker had in mind for them. You might reach various conclusions; such a pair were designed by the finest craftsmen in the world for shooting as a pair at driven game on occasions which represented the peak of that ritualised and specialised art. The life of a rough shooter's gun, dragged through hedges, exposed to mud, sand, weather, struggling through the tangle, fired at magpies and grey squirrels, might sway you to buy something less pretentious for your ramblings, and keep your best pair until you aspire to higher things or as investments.

Alternatively, your thoughts might take the line that even the most posh guns were made for using, that to keep them in an airless bank vault was as inappropriate as to use them. Why not risk the odd scuff and scratch—easily mendable anyway—and derive pleasure from using the best?

My own view is to take a gun which is of lesser, although still honest, pedigree. You will worry less about it and be able to relax more easily in its company. Try to find a single all-round weapon which will serve for all occasions. Those who take one gun for the moor, a heavier one when the odd goose might be expected and a third when walking up woodcock, will rarely shoot well with any of them. Better to stick to one, get to know it well, and use different cartridges to match the quarry and the circumstances.

It is possible nowadays to use a single gun and, by selecting the right ammunition, give yourself the right load for geese which call for a heavy load of large pellets, or snipe which call for open borings and a light load of small shot. A standard 12-bore is the most popular weapon by far and this will serve your needs. Go for the chamber length of the all-round 2¾in, which will give you the facility to use heavier ammunition and the longer-cased cartridge if you like. The shorter 2½in is for driven game shooting only and too limiting for the all-round use of the rough shooter.

Over-and-under or side-by-side is purely a matter of personal choice. Some say (I am not among them) that the side-by-side is now a little *démodé*, and there is no doubt that the over-and-under is cheaper to buy, generally of good quality and far more popular than the old-fashioned weapon. It matters little as long as it suits you. If you are lucky enough to buy a new one, and not have it passed down to you (as happens so often), then have the gun adapted to fit you. This service is not exclusive to the new gun for it can be done to a second-hand model, but the expense is one thing I would recommend and I bid you remember that rough shooting and saving cash are usually two good bedfellows.

Try wearing another man's suit or, if you live in the country, digging with his fork. Nothing beats having your gun fit you, for often you will shoot in difficult, cramped circumstances, crouched in a hide, facing foul weather or knee deep in a snipe bog. An extra and unnecessary inch on the stock means misses, frustration and disappointment.

A double barrel is vastly preferable to a single, and nowadays it is rare indeed to see a single in the field. The semi-automatic has not the adherents it had before the number of cartridges in the magazine was limited to two, but you see the odd one about. I tried one but did not care for it—a nasty bag of tricks—but its advocates defend it on the grounds of light recoil for the less robust shooter such as youngsters or frail people. The semi-auto is frowned on in company, not least because it is impossible to see whether it is or is not loaded. The old worry about having five shots as opposed to everyone else's two has been overtaken by legislation; but old prejudices die hard.

Bores smaller than 12 have their advocates. If you reflect that many rough shooters take their sport in wild country and there is much walking over desolate miles of moorland or wide acres of arable, then weight is important. Every ounce of gun you take out when fresh in the morning, is an ounce of gun you have to carry back wearily at night. Smaller bores such as the 20-bore are increasingly popular; the 16-bore is quite a rare object these days and did not catch on; the 32- and 28-bores, although they have their adherents, are not common, so the 20-bore is the most sensible alternative to the twelve.

The .410, by the way, so often advocated as a beginner's gun, is light to carry but the patterns it throws are unsatisfactory and this makes it a hard gun to shoot with accurately; too many misses for a young shot can be discouraging. The .410 is a gun for the super-pro and is not suitable for all-round rough shooting.

The 20-bore has much going for it. It can be a good pound lighter than a 12, is capable of firing a full ounce of shot, and is easy to handle and quick to point at the fleeting, rough shooter's target of a walked-up snipe, a teal flickering in the half-light or a bolted rabbit. Unlike for some small bores, the cartridges are easily available and it is often demonstrated that birds quite as high and hard as any shot with a 12 may be taken by someone who knows how to shoot. The pattern and hence the effective range are slightly less for a 20 than a 12, but when you consider how many shots you take at quite close range during a season compared with the tiny handful that stretch the barrels, this is not a factor to consider seriously.

I have used a 20-bore when walking long distances on a grouse moor and while it breaks my own rule of having one gun for all occasions, and I prefer my favourite old 12-bore for nine out of ten shooting days, there are circumstances when exceptions prove the rule. The light gun made for a much easier day over some pretty tough going.

A slip in which to keep your gun may be used to protect it from scuffs when moving from place to place on and around your shooting ground. On no account take the slip with you when shooting; it weighs too much and is awkward and will be of no use to you. For motoring, a traditional oak and leather or modern hard, crush-proof gun case is recommended. Even a modest motoring prang will ruin your gun if it is in a slip or unprotected, and the motor case is no more than sensible protection of a valuable asset in transit.

You can get a patent-leather or nylon sling which slips over the gun barrels and round the stock in a secure way to allow the gun to be carried when there is no hope of a shot and still some way to go, such as coming down from a grouse moor or walking home at the end of the day. These devices look a little flimsy and one fears that a favourite gun will somehow slip through and crash down on the stones. However, first with trepidation and later with absolute confidence I have used a carrying-sling and have never suffered a mishap. A gun is not designed for being carried for long periods and it weighs heavily after a time.

The business of fixing sling swivels to the underside of the barrels and to the stock is a dodge favoured by Continental sportsmen and is not popular in the UK. There has been an inbuilt resistance to screwing extraneous lumps of metal into stocks and barrels and the view is that sling swivels spoil the look and the line of an otherwise handsome weapon: such an operation incidentally, requires a re-proofing of the barrels. Again, this is an old prejudice but we seem to be stuck with it, and the alternative I have suggested enjoys the benefits of the sling swivel and none of its disadvantages.

The matter of chokes used to be a popular subject for discussion. Choke is the internal constriction of the last inch of a shotgun barrel which has the effect of bunching the shot and holding it together for longer, thus giving better patterns at greater range. In its day it was a significant invention, but modern thinking and new ideas have done much to reduce its importance. The fact that the great majority of shots are taken within easy shotgun range and that the grandstand, long-range ones (shots which ought not to be taken anyway) are events of once or twice a season, suggests that the pattern of the gun must be at its best for the great majority of chances rather than for rare occasions.

Thus, cry the latest experts, 'all choke is the invention of the Devil'. Open borings and small shot make for full bags. The tightly choked gun misses or smashes at close range and at long range the chance is uncertain at best so any advantage is reduced. Add to this the fact that modern cartridges can be designed to have the same effect as choke and hold the shot together by means of special wadding envelopes, and the shooter has the flexibility he needs without having to resort to carefully regulated chokes. Many over-and-under shotguns have chokes which may be changed by means of a spanner, so that full choke may be changed for improved cylinder in the time it takes to write this sentence.

If the rough shooter—and any other shooter for that matter—takes my advice he will use improved cylinder and nothing fuller than quarter choke for ninety per cent of his field shooting, and leave the fifty-metre flukes to the magnum and 8-bore men. If he makes sure of everything within thirty metres, his bags will be consistently heavier than that of the full choke disciple.

The cartridge should be matched to the quarry. The smaller and closer the target, the smaller the shot and the lighter the load you need. The favoured driven game load of an ounce of number 7, 7½ or even 8 will do for much of the rough shooter's work when the range is moderate and the target walked-up game or bolted rabbits. For shooting hares or wildfowl something rather heavier is required and here your longer chamber comes in useful. Hares are robust and large animals and can take a deal of stopping, especially when they are running away from you. Many pellets tend to run along the body under the skin without penetrating. Clean and humane kills are the duty of the sportsman.

Duck and geese have dense feathers and strong bones; they are designed to fly far and fast in all conditions so they too call for the greater shocking-power of heavier shot. However, the beginner can easily become muddled by shot sizes for this and that and weights of loads for every occasion so that he ends up in a real tangle convinced that he has the wrong cartridge in the chamber. Far more important is it that the cartridge suit the gun, and for this a simple experiment on a pattern plate will provide the evidence. Try a few loads fired at thirty yards at a steel plate set in a safe place where there is a secure background and no risk of stray pellets causing trouble, and note the density of the pattern from various proprietary brands of ammunition. You will find that one suits your gun better than the others and this consideration is more important than changing shot and cartridge length at every fresh corner.

Carrying your stock of ammunition is a matter of some importance to the rough shooter. He will not be expecting all that many shots in a day in the field walking up and carrying out his impromptu drives, but he needs enough ammunition to make sure he does not run out. Even twenty shells in a pocket can weigh heavy and awkward. Either spread your ammo between your coat pockets or, better still, carry it in a cartridge belt and distribute the weight in a way that makes it unnoticeable. The standard belt will take twenty-five 12-bore cartridges but you can get one to take thirty; various bores are catered for by the trade. Closed loops are best so that when the leather stretches, the next, vital cartridge will still be quickly available to a fumbling hand and will not have slid so far into the loop that the metal is deep into the thong. Closed loops mean that the head remains proud of the leather no matter how stretched the leather becomes.

I do not care for the belts with metal clips; purely a personal prejudice, but I have an instinct that the less metal you have about you the better. Less to scratch a precious gun-stock, less for whistle to clink against during a critical stalk when silence is golden, less to rust, stretch with wear and rub on the inside of your coat. A cartridge-bag is all right for the formal shoot when not much walking is required but it is of no earthly use for the rough shooter. If he is expecting a great many shots, at pigeons for example, spare boxes of cartridges may be carried in the game-bag. Usually I take the extra precaution of wrapping them in a polythene bag to keep the boxes dry.

There is very little else which will be useful in the way of hardware. A pocket knife is essential, advice which thirty years ago would have been superfluous, for then a man would as soon leave home without his trousers as his knife. The habit seems to have died out.

Most handy, even if you use it only once in five years, is the pull-through. A simple weight on a piece of string with a scrap of rag on the other end may be left to bide its time in the old feathers, bottle tops and sandwich packets which form a dense crust inside your game-bag. On that one day when you stumble in the mud, scoop up a wisp of snow or insert two plugs of peat into your muzzles as you negotiate a dyke, that tiny accoutrement will save your shooting day. Drop the weight down the blocked barrel, pull it through and—hey presto!

Wildfowlers and those taking their sport on coastal marshes, where tides can do nasty and unexpected things, have been advised for many years to include a whistle, torch and compass in their kit. I know that every ounce counts when you are walking great distances over difficult terrain, but like the pull-through, you might use your compass, whistle or torch but once in your life and on that occasion it just might save you from being drowned.

Your dog will need a lead unless he is rock-steady and of course the dog whistle is essential. Train your dog to the whistle rather than the human voice. The voice is frightening to game and the rough shooter ought to be blending with the countryside and not intruding into it with unnecessary noise and bellowing at unruly hounds. Game is neither deaf nor blind and a whistle is far less disturbing.

A capacious bag is vital. It was the custom once to scrounge ex-GPO mailbags and use them in the shooting field. The average rough shoot resembled an annual outing of postmen. The GPO changed the design, possibly to circumvent their being misappropriated by shooting folk, and thus a valuable source of supply was lost. The postman's bag was huge, lightweight, made of unobtrusive canvas, and had a broad and adjustable shoulder strap—all the characteristics which were unavailable in the gun shops and which we craved. All you could buy was a pretentious thing into

which you could not squeeze one good hare, with a poor little scrap of net on the front, there for show as much as anything else.

Let your bag be huge, of the sort you can get from Shooting Developments of Scotland whose 'Bag for All Seasons' and 'Bag for All Sports' incorporates the features I have identified. There is room in one for four good hares, or eighteen mallard, or seven greylags (tested and vouched for by me), so that the user's strength to carry the full bag is exceeded by its capacity. All your equipment may be carried in this bag so the separate compartment is useful, if only to keep the feathers off your sandwiches.

While many shooting folk, often those of the old school, are bound too much by tradition which may have become outdated, there is a place for dressing properly and practically; question some of the conventions by all means, but this book is not the place for such a debate. Proper clothing for shooting is a mark of respect to the quarry, your host and other people present who will have taken the trouble to turn out properly kitted. To dress down is to debase the occasion. It is sometimes the case that the conventional clothes are the most suitable, breeks being a case in point.

Plus-twos or shooting breeks are available at competitive prices from many places. They are warm, allow room for the knee to bend easily, and fit snugly about the leg, allowing wellies to be worn in comfort. The pockets are generally deep enough to prevent your treasures falling out and getting lost in the grass; the knees and seat should be double thickness and there could

Taking advantage of broken ground in winter

not be a better all-round garment for the lower limbs than the dear old breeks; they suit every shooting occasion from gun dog training to walking the moor or just pottering about on your shoot.

Breeks may be had in a variety of materials from leather to moleskin (not real moles but a special type of brushed cotton first worn by the old Victorian 'Navigators'), corduroy or hard-wearing Derby tweed. Make sure they fit properly when you buy a pair and they will last for ages and be well worth the investment.

With the breeks go long socks or stockings fastened at the knee with a garter, or better still, a tie which does not have the elastic's propensity for stopping the circulation of the blood to the feet. Some shooting stockings are made too short for a good turnover at the top. Check this before buying and also that the wool/fibre mix is right, to combine the warmth of one with the hard-wearing properties of the other. Some shooting stockings have special padded feet; these are very good and warm in the cold weather but if your boots are on the tight side the padded stockings can make them too snug.

Over-trousers may be worn in rain or when you have to walk through dense and dripping cover such as sugar-beet or kale. These are a necessary evil and most uncomfortable to wear but may be had in robust thornproof material either as stud-on leggings or as full trousers with a drawstring top. Lightweight ones in various weights of nylon are also available but many of them are not proof against thorns and certainly not against barbed wire, both curses of the rough shooter's life.

The feet are well worth taking care of: you get only one pair to see you through your life and they call for cosseting. To go out rough shooting on hill, in fen and over moor in uncomfortable footwear is a form of masochism with which it is difficult for a logical and sane person to come to terms. Modern wellingtons are good all-round boots which keep the feet dry (but do not prevent them sweating) and which may be easily removed with a bootjack and hosed down in a moment to make them as clean as new.

Some find that these are uncomfortable and chafe, and that their skin reacts badly to a long day encased in them. A good but expensive alternative is the leather-lined welly, either zipped or pull-on, of the type made by Aigle. These combine the kindness of a leather inner and the good, well tried protection on the outside which rubber affords. As for the price, my pair of leather-lined has outlasted three pairs at least of conventional wellies, so in the long run the cost is well justified.

My personal favourite for any rough shooting when there is serious walking to be considered is leather. Excellent leather boots may be had from Outdoor Pursuits centres, army surplus or mail order. Often they are imported, usually with long leg, also stitched-in tongues so that you can walk dryshod through quite deep puddles, and sprung sole, well made with good ankle support, allowing the feet to breathe and wearable for the longest day without chafing or fatigue. Cleaned, oiled and cared for, one pair will last a lifetime. I have a pair of American Golden Retriever boots (the make is no longer available), which I use exclusively on the grouse moor. They have seen twelve years' service and fit as comfortably as old gloves. Many a weary mile they and I have trudged and never have I come home wet-footed, nor have I slipped over nor twisted an ankle while those around me wearing wellies are like men trying to climb a butter mountain in pumps. Good boots are essential.

Break them in by wearing them round the house or office for a week or two; you might attract some curious glances but in comparison with the agony of wearing new boots for a ten-mile hike through thick heather this will seem such a small sacrifice as to be deemed well worth it. It is vital that leather boots are greased, waxed and cleaned every time you use them. Do not put them by the roaring fire but let them dry gently, stuffed with newspaper; this might be seen as a score in favour of the trouble-and-maintenance-free rubber, but in my view it is such a small price to pay for many advantages.

Moving up the rough shooter's body: his shirt, waistcoat and underwear are a matter for himself and it does not do to pry. Clearly he will adapt his wardrobe to suit the weather; he does not need me to tell him to come in out of the rain! Good quality long johns are excellent for the depths of winter; Damart make good ones with a long-sleeved vest to match. This gear will keep you warm on the coldest day this country has to offer; you may not need to wear it often but when you do—you bless the day you bought it.

Those quilted waistcoats or 'body warmers' are popular and good, and they allow freedom of movement while keeping the back and tummy cosy. This leads to the most important garment of all, the topcoat.

Any fool can be uncomfortable, wet and cold because he has the wrong coat for a shooting day. The days of tumbling experiments and crude technology, of India rubber, oilskin and mackintosh have long since passed, and now we are spoilt for choice. To keep warm and dry you need do no more than I did in 1963 and invest in a waxed cotton jacket of the type made famous by Barbour. My first Solway Zipper cost me £9, lasted for ages and gave good service. It became so popular that the word Barbour, like the mackintosh, passed into the language as a common noun. We almost came to love the drawbacks—the fact that a hard slog over saltings made the body as wet from trapped perspiration as from a thunderstorm. That the proofing wore in key places and let in water, but it rubbed off on car seats when fresh. The olive fading to near black was unsuitable for many shooting situations and by no stretch of the imagination did a waxproof ever look smart. And, when cold, the material was stiff and unkind. Time passed, and the problem of a breathable material was identified and addressed. What was needed was a coat which allowed the body to ventilate but also kept the rain at bay. Early experiments were mixed and we hurried back to our wax with something like relief. However, the breakthrough had to and did occur, a notable example being the development by Courtaulds of the cotton fabric, Ventile. This is long staple cotton spun into yarn, doubled for extra strength and lightly proofed. When wet from rain the fibres swell to lie tightly together allowing the body to ventilate, but keeping water out.

A classic sample of a Ventile coat is the Applejac shooting jacket from Carol Cocks of Carlisle. Well cut, extremely comfortable and handsome, it looks good in any shooting company. Pockets are capacious, the zip—often a weak point—is sturdy, there is a stud-on hood and a removable, quilted lining. A touch of class is the leather trim on handwarmer pockets, cuffs and pocket flaps to prevent wear.

An interesting variation on the theme is the general country jacket from Kate Gill of South Devon. The main design aim of the Gill Pins Country coat is comfort for the wearer in wide temperature variations, as well as in the wet. Made in a brand new cotton material called Suplesse from Thomas Mason, which has similar properties to Ventile, this jacket tackles the possibility of a saturated coat ceasing to breathe efficiently.

The jacket is made in two parts, with the sleeves being removable by means of studs, whereupon the wearer rolls them up and carries them as a backpack via ingeniously placed straps. This has useful applications for a walked-up day, especially on grouse moors where conditions can change dramatically in a short period of time. The idea is a novel one and represents a serious attempt to overcome the problems of having a coat which sees the wearer through a day when he is perspiring one minute and cold the next.

The sleeve section is attached by my *bête noir*, the dreaded press studs, but for those who feel as I do, Velcro can be substituted quite easily. Costing about £175, it is less expensive than, for example, the Applejac (which retails at around £250), and while no quality coat is cheap, a shooting jacket should be a once-in-a-lifetime buy so it is worth taking the trouble to get it right. Get the best you can afford, and don't make false economies.

Finally, there is the veritable Rolls Royce of shooting jackets, which combines the traditional quality and texture of well-cut, beautifully tailored tweed with the proven properties of Gore-Tex, a breathing membrane which allows body moisture to vent out while keeping rain at bay. The makers claim it is the most advanced weather-beating fabric available. The expanded polytetrafluoroethylene (PTFE) membrane has nine billion pores per square inch, each 20,000 times smaller than a droplet of water but 700 times larger than a molecule of water vapour. In other words, sweat, being water vapour, can vent out while rain water is kept at bay. The makers claim that, as with Ventile, Gore-Tex is used by the armed-forces.

If you take a material with these properties, hand it to a Savile Row tailor of the pedigree of Walter Norton & Son, and add to that the revered name of Boss, you end up with a shooting garment to rival the sun, the moon and the stars. The coming together of such giants on this felicitous project has produced a shooting suit which seems almost too good to take out into the mud where briar snags and rain lashes.

You need have no fear, for the superb quality tweed, quilted lining and the all-important Gore-Tex inner is proof against the worst the British countryside and weather can throw at it. What is more, the coat is redolent of that indefinable element, style. The leather trimming, softly subtle shades of the countryside, hand-woven tweed in bracken and heather-muted tones, all speak of genuine quality. The price might seem daunting to those used to buying from Millets or off-the-peg waxproofs at Sunday markets, but clobber of this calibre does not come cheaply. The Norton Gore-Tex Field jacket, off the peg, is yours for £350, while the plus twos cost £145, and are guaranteed for three years.

It costs rather more to have a bespoke suit. But this outfit is for the man who has everything and wants to spoil himself: he can cut a dash on a shooting day, feel the utmost confidence in his appearance and rest assured that whatever the weather he will remain warm and dry.

The ideal shooting coat should be warm, waterproof, not too heavy and well-fitting with adequate pockets for documents and cartridges. It should breathe, look smart, have a storm collar and cuffs, stout zips, minimal studs, be comfortable and be blessed with that vital ingredient which makes you feel good, even slightly proud, when wearing it. A shooting coat in the new materials will cost you no less than £150 and no more than four times as much. Waxproof remains popular with wildfowlers, is competitively priced and is one of the best with thorns. But, as recent developments and changing tastes have shown, there is life after wax.

A scarf, neckerchief or cravat is handy to seal the gap between chin(s) and coat collar. Hardened wildfowlers use an old towel or scrap of scratchy, army camouflage-netting, but their pelts are as tough as old leather and the run-of-the-mill rough shooter might care for something a little more gentle on his sensitive skin.

The hat to top off the ensemble is important and for more than mere show. As well as protecting the head and keeping in the warmth (most body heat is lost directly through the head), it shades the white human face from the eyes of game, passing pigeon, approaching duck or geese or any game which is driven towards you. A shooting man is not properly equipped unless he has a hat, the choice of style and material being left to his personal taste.

Gloves are useful in cold weather for no one can shoot properly, work the safety-catch or feel comfortable with cold hands. The gun often needs to be carried at the ready and there is no protection for the fingertips from the mean winds. Here again the choice is up to the shooter, but mittens are popular, or those leather gloves with a finger which peels off allowing the trigger finger to poke out when action is called for.

Thus the rough shooter from head to toe. Little extras might include an all-weather suit of fine nylon which squashes into a tiny packet, weighs practically nothing and will go on over all your clothes in the event of a sudden downpour far from home.

Common sense dictates much of what the rough shooter takes with him, but he is wise to bear in mind the old countryman's saying that 'if it looks like keeping fine, take a coat; if it looks like rain, please yourself'. He owes it to his quarry and his companions not to turn out in jeans or old gardening togs, and yet is not hidebound to the extent of the covert shooter. The balance is an important one to get right. Good boots (wellies or leather), proper stockings, breeks, waistcoat, waxproof or one of the new type of breathing coats, hat of his choice, mittens and neckerchief will see him right for almost every occasion.

Extras include game pliers or dispatchers which are useful for those not adept at dealing with wounded birds. All shooting people have an obligation to dispatch quickly and humanely any wounded bird or animal which comes to hand. Haphazard bangings and thrashings are not good enough. Unless you have the knack of doing the job by hand, which calls for practice, then a pair of pliers which deal a quick and painless nip round the neck of the bird will answer the purpose. This implement may be carried in a sheath on the belt to keep it out of the way when not needed.

Too many things hanging round your neck get tangled and can be a nuisance, and I feel that unless wildfowling binoculars have limited use, especially the large ones as used by submarine commanders in World War II and available from Milletts. Modern pocket-sized ones are much better, but just see how many times a year you actually use them and how many weary miles you carry them. Remember, every ounce counts. The dog whistle is an exception and in certain cases a duck or goose call on a neck lanyard will repay the trouble of taking it.

Calling wildfowl has for too long been the exclusive preserve of our American cousins, who are experts at the gentle art. One or two wildfowlers in the UK use the call to deadly effect but the dodge remains under-exploited. Properly blown a call can, on certain days, fill the bag which might otherwise have stayed empty. Used with decoys for geese, or mallard coming in to a pond, a call can be most effective; it can also be a famous bird-frightener if used at the wrong moment or blown incorrectly.

An acquaintance used one for years with palpable lack of success. The harder he blew the more rapidly the approaching fowl fled from the scene. It appeared that my chum had mastered only the mallard *alarm call* and this explained their reluctance to come in. Obviously he had learned that call very well, for it never failed. It is beyond the brief of this book to instruct in the fine points of calling, which for some can become a lifetime's obsession,

Opposite:
The flight shooter must wear camouflaged clothing

but books are available, as are instructional cassette tapes, from Shooting Developments in Fife, which make clear all about the calling of grey geese and duck. Modesty forbids me to mention the perpetrator of the one on calling mallard.

Food and drink should be modest but enough to keep you going. Daintily wrapped morsels of chicken or vol-au-vents are not the thing at all. All you need is a little fuel at the right moment, you are not out for a picnic which slows you down and makes you sluggish, and all the feasting should come later in the evening when you have reached journey's end. A sandwich or two will keep the wolf from the door for long periods; a small thermos of soup or coffee is better than spirits. The latter do not, contrary to popular belief, warm you up when cold; they have the opposite effect. Alcohol and shooting make ill bedfellows, but after all is over it is a different matter.

The last accessory which I recommend most strongly is the game diary, not the sort with dreary columns for recording those species of which you might shoot one in a lifetime if lucky, but more of an old-fashioned diary which records your adventures, where you went, the weather, your companions, good dog work, various happenings, beasts and birds seen and any little item which catches your fancy. This will give great pleasure in years to come, believe me because I have kept just such a book for thirty years and it is a constant delight to browse in it when the mood takes me. Who knows, after your demise at a ripe old age, someone might wish to publish it!

Finally, a check-list is handy. Nothing is worse than arriving at your destination, miles away, to find that some vital item has been left on the kitchen table. All you do is write a list on a card and stick it to the wall in your front porch, gun cupboard, by the coat-hooks, or even in your car—anywhere that will be noticed before you have set off. I have one in my little gun-room and it reads: 'Gun; Slip; Ammo; Bag; Whistle(s); Dog lead; Wallet; Specs; Food; Coat; Hat; Wellies/Boots; Shoes; Gloves; Dog.' Yes, it *is* possible to leave the dog at home; I know because I have done it.

Owning and looking after your equipment is one of the pleasures of all country sports. To take a pride in your gear, the care you lavish on it, the fact that it never breaks down or fails you, that bootlaces are renewed when worn, cartridge belts dubbined, tears in coats mended, waxproof re-dressed, gun serviced annually and always cleaned—all are symptoms of one who cares for his sport and is keen to get it right.

Any one item breaking down when you are miles up on a wild moorland or waiting for geese by a lonely firth could ruin an evening's sport and leave you feeling rueful and resentful; no need to, for it was probably nobody's fault but your own. Each of us has left things behind or had them break down on us, and each time it happens there is a determination not to allow it to happen again. The check-list is a vital aid, and since using mine my record of forgotten essentials has dwindled almost to nil.

9
The Rough Shoot Gamekeeper

Ian McCall

A good pattern

Becoming your very own gamekeeper is something that many, if not most, game shots consider they would love to do at some stage during their sporting career. Professional folk from an enormously wide spectrum of jobs find enchantment, relaxation, and an all-encompassing release-valve for their residual energy in keepering their own shoot after work hours. Others save this cherished ambition for their retirement. Many persist in pursuing the activity from youth to death, proving that for them at least it has a magic, almost a therapeutic addiction, that is too strong to kick.

Finding Ground; assessing the Potential of Unlikely Places; the Size; the Price

The urge to be your own keeper may be strong, but finding sound ground on which to practise this art becomes more difficult by the day. This is hardly surprising with more people wanting to conserve and shoot game, and the land available constantly disappearing to one development process or another.

It will pay to be as choosy as you dare from the start. The greater the number of places you look at and survey, the better your chances of finding a

155

real gem. One way to learn about ground available is to hunt through the local and agricultural press. It will probably pay for you yourself to advertise in such papers. Don't be bashful. Be prepared and proud to admit to membership of conservation organisations such the Game Conservancy, RSPB, BFSS and BASC. Acquire some references from trusted and respected local people involved in the countryside. In short, take the trouble to make people aware that you are going to be a responsible tenant. Often this fact is more important than the depth of your pocket to your potential landlord.

Other methods of hunting suitable ground include the direct approach. Door-to-door work can occasionally succeed but in these days of pressure selling this technique can be counter-productive. It may therefore be better to give your details to all the land agent companies operating in your area—buying, selling and renting land, including sporting uses, is very much their job.

Once a property is found, how do you assess its potential? Your own experience will be crucial, but in these initial stages of acquiring a shoot that you may retain for life it invariably pays to have one of the Game Conservancy's professional consultants at your side once you are seriously interested in an area of ground. Not only can such an experienced eye offer a sensible bracket of prices, but those dealing with shoot management on a daily basis can see possibilities which others simply cannot envisage. Key questions may need to be asked at this stage on future agricultural, forestry and other management matters that relate to what may be about to become your shoot.

It is a source of constant surprise just what can be achieved in sporting terms by dedicated energy and enthusiasm. One classic example is river and wildlife artist Will Garfit's seventy-acre shoot at Hauxton in Cambridge-

The rough shooter sets his own agenda for the day

Left:
Four is a good number for a rough-shooting team

Top:
An enthusiastic partner adds to the pleasure

Above:
The rough shooter is nowhere without a dog

The rabbiters return home

shire. Having purchased it at an auction when he was still a student, and when he could ill afford to become even a modest 'landowner', Will set about developing his impulse buy, a derelict gravel pit sandwiched between factories, housing estates and main roads. Having harnessed the help of several of the local residents with a bent for field sports on the aquatic side, Will systematically created a carp fishery, a trout farm, and a sporting trout fishery within his mixed shoot. The shoot itself produced ten days a season with an average bag of seventy head, much of this natural wild game! More important, the quarry listed in the bag often boasted ten or more species in a day.

So never be over-impressed by mere acres. Holding cover, nesting areas, water, woods, heather, and in a forestry situation open areas, these are the important habitats to be searching out, and the greater the variety the better. Obviously it is a bonus to have plenty of ground, but the usual custom is to sell or rent sporting rights by the acre, so the more you acquire the greater the potential cost. If the land concerned is bare grass-fields, or an intensive arable desert, it may be far from good value.

Shape should always be considered. The ideal shoot is square or even circular. Sport on long narrow strips of land can be at the mercy of the neighbours. Equally, parcels of land within your shoot that are out of bounds are an inconvenience at best and a nightmare at worst. There are more people living in the countryside than keepers who know how to operate a pheasant-catcher!

Sporting rents recorded in the Game Conservancy's Game Shooting Cost Analysis scheme vary from a bottle of best malt whisky for a charming 200-acre highland property to over £12 per acre for a marginal hill farm in Dorset with a pond and a couple of small woods. Much depends on the geographical location and the game holding and producing capacity of the land. Whatever terms you negotiate, always ensure that all the conditions are recorded in writing by both parties, including the length of the lease and when the rent is reviewable. That great game larder in the sky is crammed full of folk who devoted part of their life on earth to building up a shoot only for the landlord to reclaim it.

Liaison with the Farmer, the Landowner and Others

Field sportsmen and DIY keepers take pleasure from their management of the land. Satisfying though this is, it must never be allowed to interfere with those whose sole or primary income is derived from the ground. In particular the farmer, who may be a tenant, must be respected at all times even if not especially helpful to your cause. In practice, an opportunity will usually occur within a year or so for you to win him round. Perhaps by some help at a busy period like harvest time, or simply by keeping him posted of dodgy developments or people you spot on the ground. Mutual trust and an understanding that you can assist each other should soon be sensed by him or her.

Similarly foresters, shepherds, tractor drivers must all be won over to being part of a team. Bottles of strong liquor around Christmas may help in this respect, but careful and considerate communication are actually more important.

Don't be afraid to ask about their jobs. Much of their answer could affect your shoot. When are woods being thinned? Which fields are the roots to be grown in next year? Where do you plan to have your 'set aside' strips? Once a discussion starts on any of these subjects you may shortly have the opportunity to influence such decisions.

In some circumstances you may need to add hard cash to win your case. Often it will be money very well spent. It could provide you with holding cover in exactly the right place. Farmer, forester and shooter should always be able to operate in harmony. If the landowner is yet another party it should be very much part of his role to ensure that they do.

Time on the Job: The Keeper's Year

Part-time keepers can be divided two ways: those who can give some time to their shoot every day, and those who can only devote intermittent duty to their ground. The latter are inevitably at a significant disadvantage. The other division is between those who live on the shoot and those who have to travel to it. Again the latter are automatically handicapped. Whatever your circumstances, it will pay to recognise the limitations of them. There is nothing more depressing than seeing grand ideas and good intentions disintegrate in front of your very eyes because Father Time cuts you short. In fact, in these days of electronics many keepering jobs can be greatly helped and sometimes even done by a machine. Two examples of such technology are the automatic feeder and the All-Terrain Vehicle (four-wheeled motorbike). The former can virtually replicate daily, punctual hand-feeding, even calling birds, while with the latter checking traps or filling hoppers can be completed in a fraction of the time that 'Shank's Pony' used to take.

So what are the key periods when demands on the self-help keeper's time are going to peak? Most people will be involved in a lowground shoot where some re-stocking is necessary, so the following are some of the main requirements:

---

2 **February**

New season starts.
1 Feed residual stock.
2 Catch up for laying pen or to swap with game-farmer?
3 Build tunnel trap sites.
4 Fox control prior to nesting season.
5 Plant trees and shrubs in mild spells.

March	Continue 1, 3, 4, 5.
	6 Set tunnel traps.
	7 Pen birds for egg production.
	8 Fence off game crop areas.
	9 Begin corvid control campaign.
	10 Rabbit control.
April	Continue 4, 5, 6, 9, 10.
	11 Reduce feeding of wild stock and count wild partridge pairs.
	12 Egg collection and incubation.
	13 Sow special game crops.
May	Continue 4, 6, 9, 12, 13.
	14 Prepare rearing field and brooder units.
	15 Rear from day-old chicks?
June	Continue 4, 6, 9, 11, 12, 13, 14, 15.
	16 Release laying stock.
	17 Build new release pens.
	18 Weed control and top-dress game crops.
July	Continue 6, 9, 15, 16.
	19 Prepare existing release pens.
	20 Oversow catch cover crops.
	21 Feed duck flight ponds.
	22 Concentrate fox control around pens.
	23 Release pheasants.
August	Continue 19, 21, 22, 23.
	24 Begin pheasant feeding.
	25 Release partridge.
	26 Trim out rides and beaters' tracks in preparation for season.
	27 Arrange help so you can escape to Scotland for a day or two of grouse shooting!
	28 Check and build hides around duck pond.
	29 Check arrangements for beaters and guns for shooting days.
	30 Count wild partridges.
September	Continue 21, 24, 25, 26.
	31 Take down, disinfect and store rearing equipment.
	32 Extend range of pheasant/partridge feeds.
	33 Put up hides for partridge shoot.
October, November, December, January	Continue 21, 24, 26, 32.
	34 Feed according to shoot day plans.
	35 Constantly update plans for shoot.
	36 Run and enjoy shoots.

A crossing shot is a rare treat for a rough
shooter

Game Habitat Improvement

Whole libraries and lifetimes have been devoted to single sections of this
subject, so those seriously considering investing in improvements should
first consult the Game Conservancy. Increasingly, many of the techniques
involved are being recognised for their contribution to general wildlife
habitat, scenic beauty, and in reducing agricultural surpluses. Therefore
most are now eligible for grant aid from one or more sources. Normally
it is the landowner or farmer who must apply for such public
financial assistance.

Where existing woods are concerned, actions beyond ride trimming and
lopping the odd tree may require a felling licence from the Forestry
Commission. Planting or re-planting will probably be eligible for a grant,
and from spring 1992 the provision of a sound five-year plan for
development and improvement could attract an additional 'management
grant'.

If new woods are planned, then size, shape and site selection are all
invariably crucial to sporting potential. Design, layout and choice of species
are all important to their success and to the likelihood of grant aid.

As a general rule small woods, and especially belts, which have a large
edge-to-area ratio, are favoured by gamebirds. They are also more easily
managed than larger woods on shooting days. The other key features to

successful sporting woodlands are that they should contain plenty of open sunny areas within, but also have adequate perimeter shelter to exclude the wind.

The special game crops can be divided into four categories. First, food crops such as maize, millet, tic beans, quinoa (South American fat hen); second, cover crops such as kale, turnips, forage rape, mustard, sugar-beet, and fodder radish. Thirdly, a number of mixtures have been developed in an attempt to provide both food and cover throughout the season. The difficulty with these is that with so many different components weed control can become impossible. Finally, there are the perennial game crops, often the farm manager's delight, because in theory at least there should be no need for the annual battle against pigeons, rabbits, deer and flea-beetle over established crops. Jerusalem artichokes and canary grass are the two commonly grown perennials.

Wetlands, Ponds and Moors

Creating a pond can destroy a wetland. Be careful that you do not drain the latter when digging the former. Also remember that making a flighting pool and feeding duck to it is often a very easy process, but makes little or no contribution to their conservation in the area. In short, it is all take and no give. Also there is a limited number of duck in any area, and too many ponds may compete with each other and lead to over-exploitation of the population.

Releasing duck may seem the answer, but this too can provide problems. Reared duck can be liberated onto water areas with great ease, and where predators are controlled a pen may not even be necessary. However, skill is often required in feeding birds correctly to ensure high-flying 'wild' duck rather than overweight skimmers or even waddlers!

On the moors, habitat management is at least half of the answer to good grouse stocks. The birds need tall heather, one foot or more high for escape cover and nesting, but short heather in the form of young nutritious tips for food. Research has shown that grouse broods rarely move more than fifteen metres from tall heather. The key therefore is to provide as many small patches of young growth as possible, but close to taller vegetation. Narrow strip fires are the obvious compromise method of producing the varied food and cover habitats required.

However, the practicalities of creating such perfect conditions are more complex for the DIY keeper, due to the limitations of labour available, legal burning season, and vagaries of the British climate.

Pest and Predator Control

Because of the legal, not to mention humane, requirement to ensure that traps and snares are inspected *at least* daily, the part-time keeper is at a major disadvantage. Those living on or very near their shoot can honour the

commitments necessary for some trapping. Those who have a significant journey to make will probably be restricted to doing what they can with the gun supplemented by short sharp bursts of more intensive action during weekends and when the daylight lengthens in the spring.

Controlling predation is a much more scientific and sensitive matter today than in years gone by. The objective of the modern keeper is to tip the predator ratio in his favour just prior to and during the breeding season. This is when game is most vulnerable and predators, many of which will also have families to feed, most hungry.

Chapters and even whole books have been devoted to this fascinating and exciting section of gamekeeping and it would be an insult to try and summarise any one section in a paragraph or two. Many of the legal techniques for trapping pests and game predators are an art in themselves. Certainly a tremendous amount of satisfaction can be derived from squeaking out a stoat or outwitting a wary crow. Anyone with a sound, strong hunting instinct is likely to find this section of keeping an all-consuming passion.

Where wild game is concerned, provision of good habitat, predator control, and winter feeding are always the top three priorities.

Feeding for Game and Wildfowl

In a way, feeding is almost the last fence in the steeplechase. After all the work of spring and summer the holding and enticing of game to the desired areas is virtually the final job before the fun of the shooting. It is therefore sheer folly to try and skimp or save at this stage.

The Game Conservancy's cost analysis has a premium section, consisting of the top twenty-five per cent of shoots supplying their figures. It is no surprise that those in the premium section invariably devote more of their hard-pressed funds to winter feed than the rest.

Remember pheasants like the best. They prefer wheat and maize to other cereals. Partridges are similar but enjoy small grains, weed seeds and even cracked or kibbled corn. Duck, by contrast, are content with barley, and even the sweepings from the dresser will attract them provided they contain some nutritious grain. Also potatoes, especially if they are soft or frosted, are popular with mallard and the other dabbling ducks.

The DIY keeper's problem with feeding reverts once again to time. For best results, birds should be fed on a regular daily basis, ideally at the same time each day and with controlled quantities. While this is often possible until November, once daylight shortens and the clocks go back things become really difficult.

Fortunately, a whole host of self-feed gravity-type hoppers can be used for pheasants and partridges. Most can be made from tin cans or from plywood and are thus cheap to construct. This is important because it is crucial to have plenty of feeders. Gamebirds are 'territorial' creatures and single birds or groups can dominate a feeder. As a guide, one feeder per 10 to 15 pheasants should be provided. By scattering fresh straw around, wastage to scavengers will be reduced and the feed points themselves will become obvious and attractive to gamebirds.

For those with a deeper pocket, electronic automatic feeders may provide the answer. These can be set in key coverts to feed precise quantities, at precise times, and need only be visited to top up the hopper at weekly or fortnightly intervals. For duck flight ponds they are therefore especially suitable.

Sense of Fulfilment

Although the hours, concerns and energy expended on being your own keeper will undoubtedly drastically exceed your intentions, the whole sport of rough shooting will take on a totally different and infinitely deeper meaning. Rather than appearing with dog and gun and hoping to exercise both on a dozen or so days in the season, the mind and body will be focussed on your shoot at varying intensities throughout every single day of the year. For many this all-encompassing passion, which can consume as much as you can give it, takes over totally from shooting. The conservation of the game and other wildlife on your shoot becomes far more important to you than the few days actually harvesting the product.

Care should be taken when setting deterrents for poachers

10
Tactics

Sometimes a drive doesn't go quite right!

The rough shooter walking up birds must be aware of the advantages of approaching things in the right way. On approaching a likely field of sugar-beet it is not enough to park at the gate, leap out of the car, whistle up the dog, snatch the gun from the slip and set off, marching up and down the rows. He might blunder into a shot or two but a methodical approach will produce better results.

The wind direction is important for this as for so many other field sports. Working into or across the wind whenever possible will give game less warning of your approach and allow your dog to work the wind and pick up scent ahead of him, giving him and you good warning that a shot might be imminent. Also, birds rise into the wind so a walked-up shot would push the birds up in front of him, rising and going away, which is the rough shooter's standard shot.

The fields ought to be quartered. Methodically work your way back and forth across the wind taking about thirty-metre swathes in, say, sugar-beet, which with a good hunting-and-flushing dog ought to ensure that no game is passed over. You should be aware that game will run rather than fly once it senses your presence, and pheasants and partridges particularly will run to the end of the row or the headland, and wait there to see what happens. There is a risk with many dogs of their picking up the scent of a bird which has done just that and scuttled off ahead. The risk is that the dog will run to the end of the row, far out of range, and flush the bird or number of birds which have taken refuge there. This causes the rough shooter to administer chastisement and hop up and down uttering strange, outlandish oaths. The temptation was just too much for the dog and he cannot entirely be held to blame.

The shooter should just be aware of the possibility of this happening and either anticipate by skirting the headland first or, when his dog drops his head and sets off stone-deaf at a steady gallop, dignity must be thrown to the winds and you must gallop after him. Many and many a time have I done just that. The rough shooter ought not to stand upon his dignity. If the wind is suitable try to work across rather than down the rows, less chance of starting birds running up to the end and more chance of surprising one as you step over a ridge.

Pheasants tend to sit more tightly in wet conditions, and in thick cover or tangled ditches can take a deal of flushing. Sometimes they push themselves in so far that they cannot extricate themselves and you have a pegged bird, one which the dog has caught. In fine, dry weather the game is likely to be up and away more quickly. The opposite is true of grouse, which sit tight deep in the heather on hot sunny days and are out on the tops and away as you cross the horizon when it rains. Obviously a grouse shooter prefers the fine weather.

Develop an eye for those places where game is likely to skulk. Trial and error will teach much as will a pinch of common sense.

I was tramping the high tops of the grouse moor one August in a biting wind and not a bird did I see. In early afternoon I rounded a bluff and topped a small rise into a little valley, where due to a freak of the hill formation the

wind was cut dead and balmy sunshine played on the heather. The pain and the buffeting were temporarily over and just as I was thinking 'if I were a grouse this is where I would be', a covey sprang from my feet. Twenty metres further on was another and another. The birds from that quarter of the moor had got out of the wind and sought comfortable quarters.

On another occasion, also on the moor, it was one of those baking hot summers of which we have had our share lately. Dogs panted with lolling tongues, guns, red-faced and also with lolling tongues, clothing reduced to the bare minimum for decorum, plodded on with hope of a shot dying by the minute. The trickling streams were almost completely dry after a six-week, rainless heatwave. Here and there a spring more persistent or well fed than the rest had survived and here were the birds. Each time I came up to a 'live' beck there were grouse nearby, having come there for the water and the last scraps of green vegetation on the moor.

After two or three such experiences I realised it was no coincidence, and sought out the wet places and saw to it that I was at the ready when one appeared. That was an example of learning by doing. Lesson learned, and there to be remembered the next time there is a dry spell.

When walking up pheasants some places have a pheasanty 'feel' about them, hard to express in words. On a bitter day in the wintry Fens when the bare fields are swept by a wind from the Urals with pellets of snow on its breath, there is little point in a shooter's quartering back and forth over the chilly acres; nothing will willingly stay on them for long. However, you come upon an old-fashioned drainage dyke not cleaned out for ten years, at

a guess. A good stand of Norfolk reed tosses its feathered heads in the wind but down below the lip in the dead brown grass, the dry tangle of rushes and the nasty-looking briar and bramble patches, all is snug and warm. Any self-respecting tramp caught out by the weather would by instinct head straight to such a spot.

Get your dog to work it thoroughly, remembering the golden rule to put him in from the downwind side, and he ought to flush bird after bird. A dog needs training to work dyke bottoms; spaniels do it instinctively, but a labrador does not take to hunting so readily and tends as a breed not to care for the prickles. One of the HPR breeds can be fun in such a situation and give the shooter time to come up to the mark and not be hurried into a shot. Pheasants tend to run along the bottoms of such ditches and hedges where, on examination, you will see a well worn pathway beneath the tangle.

Very few gamebirds care to be wet. On a rainy day when the kale and sugar-beet leaves hold about half a pint of water each, which they seem intent on pouring down your boots, the birds will not be there with their feet muddy and feathers all wet. Go to the root crops in dry weather, early in the morning or late in the afternoon. In the wet, seek out the little copses, the dry, dead grass of the spinney bottoms where the wind and rain are less penetrating. In other words, use your loaf. If conditions are uncomfortable for you, it is a fair bet that they are equally uncomfortable for the quarry, so find the places where you feel warmest and there will be the pheasants.

I have mentioned the human voice in general terms and it will do no harm to emphasise the point. The human voice is a frightener of game which is neither blind nor deaf. Walk it up and harry it a time or two and it learns what is afoot and takes evasive action rather than fly and give you a shot. The cunning hunter, which is what a good rough shooter ought to be, insinuates himself in the landscape; he avoids bellowings to his dogs and instructions to his neighbours. Sound carries. He closes his car door not with a mighty bang but gently with a click. He communicates with his dog by whistle, his words are few and quiet.

Learn to be a calm, collected, unexcitable person, move slowly and with forethought, make plans and stick to them, come and go unnoticed and your bags will be far heavier than if you dash about shouting madly, overcome with the thrill of it all.

Enjoy the whole experience of being out. It is a privilege to walk the open countryside with a gun in your hand and dog at your side but you are there for more than simply to fill the bag. Be aware of things around you, of rare birds to be seen, of animal behaviour, of the swallows kissing their reflections on the surface of the duck pond, the owl mourning in the oaks. You might find a stand of mushrooms, or pause to pick a few blackberries in autumn. There might be a useful log for the fire which you make a mental note to come back for later with the saw (provided the landowner is happy), or a ground-ash stick just grown, it seems, to challenge your skills as a stick-dresser.

You will note the changing weather and the approach of new seasons, the smell in the air that tells of the onset of winter, the overblown aroma of September mornings when the dew lies heavy on rank vegetation well past

its sell-by date. The martins gather on the wires, the grey geese fly over gabbling mournfully—all these are the things of rough shooting. It is not about a man with his head down thinking only of the next shot, eager to fill his bag, to take what he can before hurrying home, oblivious of the things around him. Such a man takes his pleasures sadly.

There will be times when the rough shooter must know when to hang on and when to push ahead. When shooting in marshy country where snipe and duck are likely to be at any time, he might decide to stay put, having walked it through, in case the birds return. He might judge that this is a possibility by the time of year, the weather and his earlier observations. Teal, and to lesser extent mallard, are always likely to drop in in small parties to splashy fields, and snipe when disturbed are even more likely to give flighted shots as they come back.

The same applies to pigeon shooting at roost when the wise shooter will decide to stay rather than go on. He will have observed the undergrowth splashed with pigeon droppings to show that the birds habitually roost there; he will glance at his watch and see that in half an hour or so they ought to be returning and he will note a rising wind which will bring the birds hurrying in low rather than making endless circles out of range, and conclude that he might be in with a chance.

Woodcock too have a habit of returning whence they were flushed and if the rough shooter blunders on one in his ramblings, a wait of twenty minutes or so hidden in the scrub will sometimes prove rewarding. In other words, a judgement must be made whether to let the game come to you or to go actively in search of it. There is a time and place for each and the experienced rough shooter knows which time is right for which tactic.

Much of the magic of rough shooting lies in the unexpected. It is not often that the shooter leaves his door intent on seeking one quarry only, exclusive to all others. Even when he goes to decoy the pigeon with all the equipment needed for that, he will be aware that during the day or in one of the many

**Guns should be broken when crossing tricky
places**

lulls he might just beat out a rough corner in the next field where a rabbit
might be found. Even a man awaiting geese will take a mallard as it flies over
or, at the end of flight when disturbance does not matter, he might enjoy half
an hour with flighting pigeons or crows. In Scotland I have done it often, for
after goose time is just when the pigeon come out to feed.

What lies round the next corner? That is one of the unanswerable and
intriguing questions. You might plod on all day with a feeling of scant
chance of a shot, a feeling which grows stronger with every blank hour that
passes. Then suddenly, you blunder into them, and flush three cock
pheasants in a hundred metres of hedgerow or put a family party of mallard
out of a wet ditch and kill a right-and-left. In an instant your day is changed
from one of gloom to ecstasy.

At the end of the day it is important that certain tasks are undertaken no
matter how tired or wet the shooter might be. First he must see to the dog
and dry it with vigorous rubbing with a coarse towel to remove surplus
moisture; it does no harm to allow the dog to dry itself the rest of the way,
and too much rubbing does no good, nor does steaming it dry in front of a
roaring fire. Let it dry itself naturally and in its own good time. See that the
animal is kennelled and fed, and its skin and ears checked for thorns and
cuts.

Next the gun must be cleaned and put away. Recent legislation places a
heavy burden of responsibility on the gun owner to keep his weapons safe,

and it is no longer good enough to say, 'I'll put it away in the morning'. Clean off all moisture and dirt inside and outside and put the gun in your chosen place of safety.

Hang up any shot game. It might not look too presentable as you remove it from the bag, and it is worth remembering that you might need to present it to a kind host or friendly farmer and therefore it should look its best. I try always to pack birds neatly into the shoulder-bag, head under one wing, tail sticking out of the top and not screwed round in a crumpled circle. It is good to take a pride in presentation of shot game, and too often a fine pheasant is stuffed into the bag any old how and comes out having stiffened into a nightmarish shape which does no one much credit and gives little pride.

A game larder sounds rather posh and has connotations of the great estates with serried ranks of hooks in a purpose-built stone palace, but ten nails hammered into a cool passageway, shed or garage wall will do. I have such a spot in the lee of my garage out of the sun and high enough to prevent dogs and cats leaping up and savaging my game. Birds and animals may be hung here safely until ready for the kitchen; they look good, air circulates freely round them and it is the proper way to do things.

A friend of mine is very keen on all sorts of shooting. His game larder is of the type described above, but he has enclosed it in that fine-mesh wire of the type used in the old-fashioned meat safe. This has the advantage that the flies cannot get at his birds in the hot weather, a real problem with September mallard, grouse and early partridge. So that he is certain of taking the latest game shot when it is needed in the kitchen, he has six cards marked with the days of the week which he places over the heads of each batch of game so that he can tell in an instant which is the freshest and which needs to be eaten up.

Hang up your outdoor clothes and clean the worst of the mud off your boots. Last of all, and very important in my view, is to write up your shooting diary. This is not one of those tedious ledgers popular on great estates in Victorian times which recorded your bag of red stags and capercaillie, but a simple and substantial diary in which to remind yourself of happy times, of companions, events, weather changes, good shots, things which went wrong, clever (or naughty) dogs, rare birds encountered and all the things which go to making a shooting day. Even blanks should be written up, otherwise you are as good as saying that the one and only purpose of going out at all is to shoot something. To the true rough shooter, wildfowler and pigeon decoyer this is not true. It is possible to enjoy a day at the end of which the game-bag flaps emptily.

It is important to take account of wind direction and strength, especially when wildfowling. We have seen how important it is for dog work and for flushing gamebirds into it, while for pigeon-roost shooting and many forms of duck and goose shooting its strength can bring birds within range and give the fowler a rare chance. The wind can also alter flightlines. A steady gale from left or right will cause birds, be they duck, geese or pigeon, to crab across it rather like someone swimming across a powerful river and hitting the bank many yards downstream of where he intended.

If the fowler awaits geese roosting on mud-flats in front of his position, birds which he knows intend to fly slap over his head to feed on the field inland of the sea wall, he must make allowance for a sideways wind. A strong one will cause him to calculate the point at which the geese will cross the marsh and he must hide there. An early flighting party will give him an indication, as will passing gulls, of how accurate are his calculations. It is not too late then to move.

Never be afraid to move. All shooters and field sportsmen generally ought to be adaptable and able to change their minds as and when new conditions dictate, and this applies especially strongly to one in a hide, no matter how carefully or painstakingly constructed. If it turns out to be in the wrong place or the wind changes or you have got it wrong, then tough luck, but up sticks and MOVE.

Beyond these wise saws and modern instances there is little further tactical advice which will be of help. The nature of rough shooting is that its decision-making and tactical planning are part of the magic; they are learned by trial and frequent failure and by getting to know your ground and the likely escape routes of every bird and beast in it. It is to be hoped that already you possess some instinct for this, a certain 'feel' for the countryside and the movements of the birds and beasts. A wise man knows where 'they' will be today and where 'they' will be likely to be tomorrow afternoon if this weather holds. When you reach that stage, you will be able to call yourself a tactician.

The real pleasure comes when you get it right. The tangible result is completely immaterial since a miss or a hit are all the same in ten years' time, but when you plan to drive your only covey of grey partridges in a certain direction, and if after a long stalk and skilful placing of the available personnel it all works, that is cause for a certain amount of self-congratulation. If you see the geese and watch them long enough to hide by the right bush on the right morning and shoot two of them—what more need be said?

11
From Bag To Table

Angela Humphreys

Endangered species

At the end of a day's rough shooting you are likely to take home a very mixed bag of game. Hopefully there will be a brace of young, cleanly shot pheasants, perhaps a wigeon, hare, the odd pigeon or two and if you are really fortunate a snipe or woodcock. You will certainly also have birds in less than perfect condition; a heavily shot pheasant, one with a broken leg or tail feathers missing. But whatever the state of the bag, it must be sorted, hung properly and prepared for the table or freezer.

Carry birds very carefully in a game-bag, preferably with a net pocket to allow the air to circulate. If returning to base for lunch, hang the morning's bag in a cool place, under cover if possible to protect it from sun or rain. At the end of the day stow the game carefully in your vehicle away from the dogs and not hidden under a pile of coats and wellies.

Hanging

Sort and hang the bag as soon as you get home. There is no correct length of time to hang game; individual taste, the condition of the game and the weather are all factors to be considered. Choose a place that is cool and airy and high enough to be out of reach of the neighbour's cat. A game larder or a piece of muslin is useful in blowfly time. Birds should be hung singly by the

177

neck, and hares and rabbits by the feet. Empty the crops of pigeons if they have been feeding on greens and paunch rabbits before hanging. Any game that has been heavily shot should be prepared as soon as possible as it will deteriorate quickly.

In warm, humid weather game need only hang for two or three days, but it may need as long as a fortnight in colder conditions. If you have driven several hundred miles with a brace of grouse in the boot you may decide to dispense with hanging altogether. Generally speaking, if the flesh between the legs and breast is still white, the bird is not high, but if it is a greenish-blue colour it is well hung!

Off with Feathers and Fur

As well as a large box or dustbin lined with a large polythene bag, have ready a small sharp knife, a pair of kitchen scissors or secateurs, a meat cleaver, a stout chopping-board, and a bucket for innards, heads, feet and so on.

Plucking and Drawing

Pluck out of doors if possible. Start with the wings, then the neck and work down to the tail and legs. Care must be taken to avoid tearing the breast skin; hold it taut and pull out only a few feathers at a time. Soft, downy duck feathers may be removed by rubbing with the ball of the thumb. As duck wings are very tedious to pluck and have very little meat on them it saves time to remove them with secateurs.

Place the bird on the chopping board.
Cut off the head at the top of the neck, slit down the neck with a sharp knife and pull away the loose skin, but do not cut it off.
Pull out the crop and windpipe and cut off the neck close to the body.
Make a cut round the vent and remove it.
Hold the bird firmly with one hand, place two fingers of the other hand inside the body cavity and draw out the intestines, heart, gizzard, liver and gall-bladder.
Discard the intestines and the gall-bladder which must be cut away from the liver.
Keep the liver, neck, heart and gizzard, which should be split and cleaned in cold water. Use the liver for pâté and the rest for stock or gravy.
Cut the skin around the foot joint, twist to break the joint and pull hard to remove the tough sinews and tendons. These will be more noticeable in a pheasant than other gamebirds.
When dressing *duck* it is a good idea to remove the two oil glands on the upper side of the parson's nose, as they may give a musky flavour to the meat.
Traditionally *waders* are plucked but not drawn, apart from the gizzard, which should be removed. Make a small cut above the thigh but below the breastbone, and with one finger locate and hook out the gizzard.

Skin the head and remove the eyes. Leave the feet on.

Skinning

If a bird has been badly damaged it is much quicker to skin than pluck. Cut off the head and clip off the wings and legs with the secateurs.

Lay the bird on its back and with a sharp knife cut lightly along the breastbone and peel the skin and feathers off in one piece. If only the breast meat is required, simply peel back the skin to reveal the breast, then, with a sharp knife, make a cut under the lower end of the breastbone. Cut deeply along the ribs close to the wings and then, using secateurs, cut through the collar bones.

Remove the breast in one piece on the bone.

Here is an even quicker method of removing pigeons' breasts:

Break each wing as close to the breast as possible.

Holding the bird head down over a bucket, tear off the crop. Don't worry if the head comes off too.

Insert both thumbs into the cavity you have made at the base of the neck and, as if breaking a tough bread roll, break the bird in half along its length.

Continue the process by peeling off from the rear the thick breast skin with feathers attached.

In one hand you have the backbone, entrails, legs, tail and breast skin which should be dropped into the bucket, and in the other the whole breastbone with a few stray feathers stuck to it. Rinse these off under cold running water.

When skinning a *hare* try to keep the fur off the flesh.

With a meat cleaver, chop off the feet.

With the head away from you, pinch up the belly skin and with a sharp knife make an incision, taking care not to penetrate the body cavity.

Cut the skin around the back legs just below the tail. You can then work the skin off the hind legs.

Turn the hare round and draw the skin off the body and forelegs by pulling it towards the head.

Cut off the head and discard together with the whole skin.

Using kitchen scissors, cut from the fork between the legs up to the rib cage.

Cut carefully through the paunch, draw out and discard the intestines.

Keep the kidneys and liver, after carefully removing the gall-bladder.

Cut the diaphragm and draw out the pluck, discarding the lungs but keeping the heart for stock.

At this point, if you wish to keep the blood to thicken a sauce or gravy, pour any that has collected in the ribcage into a basin.

With a sharp knife remove the thin membrane which surrounds the meat.

Young hares may be left whole for roasting or cut into joints.

Divide the saddle into four even-sized joints. The front legs should be left whole but the hind legs may be divided at the joint.

For a whole saddle of hare remove all four legs and trim away the loose belly-skin and the ribcage.

Soak the meat for twenty-four hours in cold salted water before cooking or freezing.

Rabbits should be paunched as soon as they are cool.

First 'thumb' the rabbit towards the vent to expel any urine from the bladder.

Using a sharp knife, cut the belly skin from vent to sternum and remove the intestines and stomach.

To skin a rabbit, lay it on a chopping-board with its hind feet towards you.

Start with the hindquarters by pulling the loose belly skin firmly towards you, peeling it off around the tail and hind legs.

Pull the legs out of the skin.

Cut off the feet with secateurs at the heel joint and remove the tail.

Turn the rabbit round and work the skin up over the head, pulling the front legs out.

Cut off the front feet with secateurs and the head with a sharp knife.

The head and complete skin may then be discarded.

Cut the diaphragm, which encloses the heart and lungs inside the ribcage.

Keep the heart but discard the lungs.

Remove and keep the kidneys and liver, which, together with the heart, may be used for stock.

Joint the rabbit unless you wish to cook it whole.

Wash the rabbit in cold water, then leave to soak overnight in cold salted water.

Rinse again before cooking or freezing.

Fit for the Freezer

Many people prefer to eat only fresh, seasonal food, but faced with pounds of broad beans or enough pigeons to feed an army, freezing what is surplus to immediate requirements makes good housekeeping sense!

Here are a few tips on freezing game:

Don't freeze game in feather or fur; they take up too much space.

Depending on the weather and personal taste, game should be hung before freezing; with the exception of wild duck, as the flavour does not improve with hanging.

Birds should be plucked and drawn or skinned, except for waders which should be plucked but not drawn.

Rabbits and hares should be skinned, left whole or jointed and soaked overnight in cold salted water before freezing.

Wipe the game with a clean cloth or paper towels and remove any visible shot.

Wrap any sharp or protruding bones in foil and pack in heavy gauge polythene bags.

Expel all the air and seal the bag tightly.

Individual rabbit joints, whole breasts or legs may be frozen separately on a baking-tray and then stored together in one large polythene bag so that you may choose the exact amount you need for a recipe.

Label the bags clearly, indicating the species, the age and the date.

Gamebirds, rabbits and hares will keep for up to a year, wildfowl for six to nine months.

Casseroles may be stored for about three months, soup for two months, but do not add eggs or cream until reheating.

Game pies may be frozen but the pastry tends to flake once thawed.

Pâtés may be frozen for two months but they must be thawed slowly and completely before use.

Frozen game may be thawed, cooked and then frozen again.

Finally, use in reverse order of storage and plan to have room in the freezer at the start of the new season.

Cooking the Bag

Grouse

In sporting circles, August is considered to be a quiet month; the Game Fair has come and gone, and the world, his wife and children are on their annual pilgrimage to the 'Costas'. But you and the dog will have had a far from quiet month as you extend the daily stroll down the field to a five-mile brisk walk with one hundred step-ups each time you come to a stile (for you, not the dog), as you prepare for the highlight of the month, tramping the moors of Yorkshire or Scotland at the start of the grouse shooting season.

Remove birds from the game-bag as soon as possible and hang in a cool airy place. A day or two is enough at the beginning of the season, but this may be extended to a week in October or November.

For successful cooking it is important to know the age of the birds. Young grouse have pliable feet, smooth legs and the tip of the breastbone is soft. The lower mandible should break if held between thumb and first finger. Older birds have scaly legs with sharp claws and the tip of the breastbone is hard and sharp. Grouse feed on heather and berries and have a unique flavour. Young birds are best plainly roasted with bacon and served with cranberry, rowan or elderberry jelly. Birds of a doubtful age need longer cooking with vegetables such as onions and mushrooms and plenty of stock or wine, until the meat begins to fall from the bones.

Grouse Parcels
Serves 4

This is a simple way to cook young birds either under a grill or outside on a barbecue.

> 2 young grouse
> 4 rashers bacon
> 4tbsp rowan or elderberry jelly

Split the grouse in halves using game shears or kitchen scissors. Remove any remaining innards and trim off any small rib bones. Wrap a rasher of bacon round each grouse half and place flesh side up on a square of foil. Put a tablespoon of jelly on top then wrap and seal the foil parcel.
Cook over hot coals or under the grill for about 30 minutes. Serve with assorted salads and granary bread.

Pheasant

The best known and most easily recognised gamebird, the brightly coloured cock pheasant and the less conspicuous hen were introduced to Britain, some say, by the Romans.

In warm weather hang pheasants for three days, and for up to two weeks in cold conditions.

A young cock pheasant has rounded spurs which become sharper with age. A young hen has soft feet which later become rough and hard.

Pheasants are surely the most versatile of all game in the kitchen. Young roasted birds make a splendid dish decorated with tail feathers, cranberries and watercress, and served with bacon rolls, fried breadcrumbs or game chips. Slivers of breast meat may be cooked in a wok with stir-fry vegetables and a sweet and sour sauce, or try whole pheasant breasts gently poached in a creamy mushroom or asparagus sauce.

Older birds may be braised with wine, cider or stock on a bed of vegetables in a chicken brick or roasting-tin with a lid, or used in endless variations of casserole, curry, pie, terrine and soup.

Pheasant with Celeriac Sauce
Serves 4

In January there are likely to be plenty of mature cock birds in the bag, as hens are preserved to ensure a good stock of wild birds for the next season. Slow cooking is needed to be sure of a tender bird. Celeriac is similar in flavour to celery. It can be grated raw for salads or cooked as a flavouring for soups and casseroles. Here it is cooked with the pheasant and then liquidised to thicken the delicately flavoured sauce.

> 1 mature cock pheasant
> 675g (1½lb) celeriac, peeled and sliced
> 300ml (½pt) chicken stock
> 150ml (¼pt) white wine
> 2 cloves garlic, crushed
> 4tbsp single cream
> Salt and black pepper
> 225g (8oz) *fromage frais*
> Chopped chives

Place the pheasant breast down in a flameproof casserole.
Add the stock, wine, crushed garlic, salt and black pepper and cook in a moderate oven (160°C/325°F/gas mark 3) for 1½ hours.
Remove the pheasant from the casserole and add the sliced celeriac.
When the bird is cool enough to handle, remove the meat from the breast in large pieces, pull off the legs and wings and leave them whole.
Return all of the meat to the casserole and cook for another hour or until the celeriac is tender.

Transfer the meat to a shallow serving-dish, cover and keep hot.

Purée the celeriac in a food processor, then return to the casserole with the cream.

Heat the sauce through gently and adjust the seasoning if necessary.

Add the chopped chives to the *fromage frais*.

Spoon the sauce over the meat and serve with glazed carrots and jacket potatoes topped with the *fromage frais*.

Snipe, Woodcock and Golden Plover

Although the snipe is only half the size of a woodcock or golden plover, for culinary purposes these waders may be treated in a similar way.

Waders should be plucked, heads skinned and eyes removed, but not drawn, except for the gizzard which should be removed. To do this make a small cut in the side above the thigh but below the breastbone, then use the index finger to locate and hook out the gizzard. This is, of course, a matter of personal taste, and birds may be drawn if preferred.

A couple of woodcock or plover will serve two people for a main course; a couple of snipe provide a splendid starter or a sumptuous breakfast for two.

The following recipe is the traditional way to roast any of these highly sought-after gamebirds.

> A couple of snipe, woodcock or golden plover
> 4 rashers streaky bacon
> 2 thick slices bread
> Oil for frying
> Juice of half a lemon or 2tbsp calvados
> Lemon wedges and parsley for garnish

Wrap two rashers of bacon round each bird.

Place in a small roasting-tin and cook in a hot oven (220°C/425°F/gas mark 7), basting once or twice, until cooked through and tender. (Approximately 40–45 minutes for woodcock, 35–40 minutes for golden plover and 30 minutes for snipe.)

The 'innards' known as 'trail' will slowly melt and mingle with the cooking juices.

Heat the oil in a pan and fry the slices of bread until crisp and golden. Drain and place on a hot serving-dish.

Place the birds on the croutons, add the lemon juice or calvados to the pan and heat through.

Pour the juices over the birds, decorate with lemon wedges and parsley and serve at once.

Opposite:
The woodcock, a prize indeed for a rough shooter

Wildfowl

Most likely to feature in the rough shooter's bag are the medium-sized wigeon and the Canada goose, the largest of the grey geese which may be shot in Britain.

There is no need to hang wild duck, though in cold conditions geese may hang for as long as two weeks depending on weather conditions and their age. This is not always easy to judge, especially later in the season; a young bird will have a flexible underbill, brightly coloured legs and notched tips on its tail feathers. If in doubt, treat the bird as old!

An apple, orange, onion or herbs may be placed in the body cavity, and as duck and geese usually have some natural fat on them they are best roasted on a rack; any excess fat may then be poured off halfway through cooking. At this point wine, cider or stock may be added. Serve with a stuffing of chestnuts or sage and onion and a prune and apple sauce. Red cabbage baked with apples and cinnamon complements both duck and goose.

Use older birds for casseroles, game pies and pâté.

Waste-Not Wigeon
Serves 4 generously

This recipe is for the cook in a hurry; it uses the breast meat only so there is no need to pluck the birds, and it takes less than 20 minutes' cooking in the microwave.

> 2 brace wigeon
> 8 rashers streaky bacon
> 100g (4oz) mushrooms, chopped
> 8tbsp sage-and-mint jelly
> 300ml (½pt) chicken stock
> Fresh sage for garnish

Skin the breast area of the birds and with a sharp knife cut away the whole breast meat on either side of the breastbone.

Cut a pocket in each breast and insert a tablespoon of sage-and-mint jelly.

Wrap a rasher of streaky bacon round each breast and arrange in a shallow dish.

Sprinkle the chopped mushrooms over the meat and pour over the stock.

Cover with clingfilm and cook in the microwave on medium for 18 minutes (or Auto Sensor: A5).

Decorate with the sage and serve with rice or noodles and a green salad.

Celebration Goose
Serves 6

A young Canada goose makes a change from the more usual festive fare of turkey or domestic goose and is perfect for Christmas or New Year.

> 1 young Canada goose, 2.7–3.6kg (6–8lb), oven-ready
> 100g (4oz) dried apricots
> 100g (4oz) fresh breadcrumbs
> 50g (2oz) chopped walnuts
> 2tbsp orange juice
> Salt and black pepper
> 150ml (¼pt) red wine
> Watercress for garnish

Soak the apricots in water for two hours. Drain and cut into small pieces.
Add the chopped walnuts, breadcrumbs, orange juice and black pepper and mix well.
Place the stuffing in the body cavity of the goose.
Tie the legs together and then take the string round the parson's nose, closing the cavity as much as possible.
Sprinkle the bird on both sides with salt.
Place the goose breast side down on a rack in a roasting tin.
Cook at 180°C/350°F/gas mark 4 for 1½ hours.
Turn the goose over, baste with half of the red wine and cook for another 1½ hours, by which time the juices should run clear and the bird should be crisp and brown.
Place the goose on a serving-dish and keep hot.
Skim any excess fat from the pan.
Add the rest of the wine to make a thin gravy.
Adjust the seasoning if necessary.
Decorate the goose with the watercress and serve the gravy separately.
Serve with roast potatoes, glazed carrots, red cabbage and Brussels sprouts with chestnuts.

Moorhen

Like wild duck, moorhen taste best when they have been feeding on stubble.
  It is much easier to pluck a moorhen while it is still warm, as once cold it is difficult to remove the black down from the breast and back. It may then be treated like wigeon or teal. If the bird proves too difficult to pluck simply remove the breast meat only and cook like pigeon, or add to an assortment of game for a pie or casserole.

Pigeon

In ones and twos, sixes and sevens or by the sackful, pigeons will surely feature in every bag!

Pigeon do not need to be hung like other game but should not be left in a sack or a jumbled heap. If you are not able to prepare them immediately for cooking or the freezer, empty the crops if they have been feeding on greens and lay the birds on concrete in the shade or in a garage, or hang them by the neck in a cool place.

I have already described various methods of plucking and skinning pigeons. It is well worth completely plucking young birds, or squabs, which are best between August and October. They are tender and succulent and may be roasted plain or with herb-flavoured cheese, sausage meat or a fruit-and-nut stuffing.

Cover the breasts with streaky bacon to prevent the fatless meat from drying. Whole breasts may be cooked quickly like beefsteak and served while still pink, or thinly sliced and cooked in a wok with stir-fried vegetables.

Older birds require a longer cooking method and benefit from marinating overnight in wine, oil and herbs. They may then be pot-roasted or casseroled with a variety of seasonal vegetables, or made into pies or pâté.

Prior's Pigeon Pie
Serves 4

It is a good idea to cook the meat for a pie on the bone as this enriches the gravy. The breastbones are discarded before filling the pie.

> 4 whole pigeon breasts
> 4 rashers streaky bacon, chopped
> 225g (8oz) button mushrooms
> 1 clove garlic, finely chopped
> 150ml (¼pt) red wine
> 150ml (¼pt) beef stock
> 4tbsp chopped parsley
> 2tsp chopped fresh thyme
> 25g (1oz) flour
> 1tbsp elderberry jelly
> Salt and pepper
> 225g (8oz) flaky pastry
> 1 egg, beaten

Place the pigeon breasts, wine, stock and chopped garlic into a saucepan. Bring to the boil and simmer gently for 1½ hours.

When cool, remove the meat from the bone and cut each breast into four slices.

Place a funnel in the centre of a pie-dish.

Add the meat and mushrooms.

Thicken the gravy in the saucepan with the flour, add the elderberry jelly and chopped herbs and season to taste.

Pour the gravy over the meat, cover with flaky pastry and brush with beaten egg.

Bake at 200°C/400°F/gas mark 6 for 40 minutes.

Serve with creamed potatoes and red or white cabbage.

Rabbit and Hare

Rabbit has been highly valued as meat fit for the table of monarchs, archbishops, lords and peasants since Norman times. Ordinary country folk preferred rabbit to hare as it was much easier and cheaper to prepare. Hares have been hunted for food for centuries, and were often poached and sold to the gentry who could afford the expensive ingredients required to make the meat palatable.

Pound for pound, rabbit and hare have more protein than beef or pork and one quarter the fat content.

I have already described how to hang rabbits and hares, to remove their jackets and prepare them for cooking. Soaking overnight in cold salted water will tone down the strong flavour of hare and help to remove the excess blood from flesh badly damaged by shot.

Leverets and young rabbits may be roasted whole, or jointed and grilled with barbecue sauce. When more mature, they are ideal cold-weather fare cooked with plenty of seasonal vegetables in casseroles, puddings and pies. They also have an international appeal, making delicious curries, sauces for pasta or served sweet and sour with noodles or rice.

Oriental Rabbit
Serves 4

1 young rabbit
1 clove garlic, crushed
2tbsp white wine vinegar
2tbsp soy sauce
1tbsp brown sugar
1cm (½in) piece fresh ginger, grated
Oil for frying
4 spring onions, finely chopped
100g (4oz) mushrooms, sliced
1 red pepper, deseeded and thinly sliced
350g (12oz) bean sprouts
50g (2oz) cashew nuts
250g (8oz) instant noodles
450ml (¾pt) chicken stock
25g (1oz) cornflour
Apricot or mango chutney
Chopped parsley

Cut the meat from the rabbit in thin slices.
In a bowl, combine the garlic, vinegar, soy sauce, sugar and ginger. Add the rabbit meat and leave overnight to marinate.
Heat the oil in a wok or large frying-pan and soften the spring onions, mushrooms and red pepper.
Blend the cornflour with the stock and add to the pan together with the rabbit and marinade.
Simmer for ten minutes stirring gently.
Place the noodles in a bowl and cover with boiling water.
Add the beansprouts and nuts to the wok and cook for five minutes, stirring frequently.
Drain the noodles, add to the wok and mix thoroughly.
Spoon onto very hot plates, sprinkle with chopped parsley and serve with apricot or mango chutney.

Quanea Hare Pudding
Serves 6

1 hare, jointed
225g (8oz) bacon, chopped
1 large onion, finely chopped
2tbsp flour
150ml (¼pt) red wine
450ml (¾pt) beef stock
2tbsp fresh mixed herbs

2tbsp made mustard
1tbsp redcurrant jelly
100g (4oz) mushrooms
Salt and black pepper
For the suet crust:
350g (12oz) self raising flour
1tsp baking powder
175g (6oz) grated suet
1tsp dried thyme
1tsp salt
175ml (6fl oz) cold water

In a flameproof casserole, blend the flour with the stock and bring to the boil, stirring until thickened.

Add the wine, hare joints, chopped bacon, onion, redcurrant jelly, mustard, herbs, salt and pepper.

Cover the casserole and simmer on a low heat for 2 hours.

Adjust the seasoning and allow to cool.

Remove the meat from the bones and return to the casserole with the mushrooms.

Sift the flour and baking powder, add the suet, thyme, salt and enough cold water to make a soft dough. Knead lightly.

Use three-quarters of the pastry to line a 1.2l (2pt) pudding basin.

Place the hare mixture in the pudding basin and add gravy to within 2.5cm (1in) of the top.

Keep the remaining gravy.

Fold the surplus pastry over the filling and dampen the edges.

Use the remaining pastry to make a lid, pressing the edges together to make a tight seal.

Cover with greaseproof paper and foil and secure with string tied round the edge of the basin.

Steam in a large saucepan for 1½ hours, topping up the water as necessary.

Serve with the gravy, creamed potatoes, glazed carrots and a green vegetable.

12
Odd and Sods

A nice right and left

Insurance

Mention has been made of the insurance which comes with the membership package of at least two of the named associations involved with shooting. It is most important that all shooting folk are protected in this way before venturing out. Any sport involving guns and of an intrinsically volatile and sometimes *ad hoc* nature like rough shooting carries an element of risk, no matter how carefully conducted.

There is always the risk of a careless shot—and who can claim not to have fired at least one in their lives? There is the risk of people being where they ought not to be and while nobody shoots where he cannot see (one of the golden safety rules), the countryside is becoming a crowded place where courting couples, children, picnickers and bird-watchers aspire to the most remote and forgotten corners and lurk behind bushes in the very places where you come to find your sport.

The risks of an accident to yourself and to others in your party are real and it is no good taking the view that it can never happen to you. One day it just might be your turn, and insurance is a prudent requirement in such circumstances. It is a personal view only, but I foresee the time when insurance will be a prerequisite of holding a shotgun certificate. It is a rule on my own shoot that every member is properly protected, and I am not happy shooting in company which includes uninsured people. They might be the loveliest, kindest, sweetest people in the world but.....

Books and Magazines

It is important for the shooting man to involve himself deeply in his sport but it can be overdone. Some shooting households have pheasant transfers glued onto every moveable object, the salt and pepper pots are in the shape of gamebirds, ducks fly across every picture, the table-mats depict archaic shooting scenes and as for their Christmas cards, it goes without saying what theme they favour.

It is proper that the shooting family involves and immerses itself at many levels with its sport, for this is the sign of a true enthusiast. The periodical magazines are not cheap but it is well worth subscribing to at least one. *Shooting Times* is perhaps the best known and certainly the oldest, being a weekly concerned entirely with shooting matters including gun dogs and clay shooting. There are many others, each with its own particular flavour. Each time it comes thudding through the letter-box the reader is informed of the changes which assail his sport at bewildering speed and often with complete unexpectedness.

It is essential to be properly informed about new legislation which affects shooting and the countryside generally. Some new moves will be on the EC front where many decisions which affect country sports will be made, and the readers are alerted whenever it is felt necessary for the shooting world to rise up and protest about some piece of nonsensical legalistic mumbo-jumbo even more crass than the rest, and belabour his MP with letters outlining his views. Sad but true: that is the world the shooting man today inhabits.

In addition, the magazines carry much to amuse, educate and entertain. It gives great pleasure to read of fellow sportsmen in other places and the adventures they have, the problems they encounter, the oddities, the solutions, the disappointments and successes. Advertisements tell the reader what is on the market and at what prices; new guns and equipment are reviewed and should he wish to buy himself a day or two of shooting at almost any level, the classified ads will have just the thing.

There are many books on shooting and the countryside on the market and all shooting men I know have collections, ranging from a handful of volumes to whole walls covered with serried ranks of every word written on the subject since man first put pen to paper. Shooting books fall into three categories, the how-to-do-it, the nostalgic and the antiquarian. Some contain elements of more than one. Which to go for is purely a matter of personal choice, but I find I need only so many of the 'How to…' sort; the information tends to date and some of them find it hard to say anything new.

Books which extol the magic of the sport and tell of great days are the ones I enjoy best. Many of the older books are in short supply and command high prices on the second-hand market, and like all collecting the bug can bite deeply, but still it is possible to pick up the odd bargain at church jumble sales.

Pictures fall into a similar category, and it is good that the shooting man should adorn his walls with works of art which remind him of his favourite sport. There are some superb sporting artists currently working and while their work is not cheap—and nor should it be—to buy an original picture, hang it and enjoy it for many years thereafter is an act of faith which the purchaser will never regret.

There are many shooting videos available. This is the new means of easy communication and should not be overlooked. Many of the associations use video as a training aid, and there are many on the market covering most aspects of country sports.

Game Fairs, from the main CLA Game Fair held annually at the end of July on a notable estate, plus the many local events which have become so popular in recent years, provide the opportunity for the rough shooter to meet those of similar interests, look at trade stands to see what is new on the market, try his dog or his shooting skills in any of the friendly competitions, seek advice from the experts on hand, and generally have an enjoyable day out.

Joining the Band—a Welcome to the Club

It is a sad fact of life that all country sports are suffering from crises of public opinion and pressures in various shapes and forms. As we have drifted more towards the towns and left behind our rural roots to the extent that not one child in a hundred can tell wheat from barley, we have forgotten the hunting instinct, and overlook the fact that supermarket birds and meat once bore feathers or hide. Questions are asked, flak is fired, and it has become necessary for shooting folk to band together into organisations which do much to protect the sport in different ways.

It is on oft-commented-on regret that too many organisations have sprung up to carry out this task, so that shooting folk are puzzled to know which one to join and which of them is the right one for him. The result is a fragmented and occasionally uneasy alliance and uncertain public stance, expensive for those who decide to join more than one, and duplicating many areas where things need to be done. However, the best and largest three, each of which has different strengths, are as follows:

The British Association for Shooting and Conservation (BASC) Formally known as WAGBI (the Wildfowlers Association of Great Britain and Ireland), the BASC is the voice of the general shotgun shooting man and woman. Based at Marford Mill in Rossett it has a large staff which keeps a watching brief on the political scene, publishes much material of use to the shooting world and exerts political pressure when and where it is needed. It runs a conservation and research programme, loans money for marsh purchase and maintains a high profile at the CLA Game Fair and at regional events. Membership attracts various privileges including third party insurance against accident which is essential for all shooting folk before even they venture outside armed with a gun.

The Game Conservancy Based in Hampshire, this body is a registered charity and as such does not enter the political arena. Instead it has concentrated on the problems of gamebirds and game animals, and has established a staff of scientists of international reputations and undertaken a series of research projects which have taught us much about what makes gamebirds tick, what they like, how to improve their lot and, by so doing, improve the quality of the countryside in which we live and take our sport.

The pressure point is created almost entirely by a farming system on which huge demands to produce more and more were made; the result was a countryside almost bereft of wild flowers (weeds), insects (pests), birds (destroyers of crops) and hedgerows (valuable growing space for more barley). It was due largely to this that may wild gamebirds diminished, especially the grey partridge which has become the symbol of the Game Conservancy.

This organisation offers professional guidance to members needing advice on how to improve the potential of their ground. Practical help and down-to-earth tips for everyone involved in shoot management, be it a few acres of rough ground which can be improved by a little suitable planting, some feed hoppers and basic vermin control, or a formal shooting estate of thousands of acres.

The British Field Sports Society (BFSS) This body covers not only shooting but hound sports, falconry, coursing and fishing. Traditionally seen as the representative of the hunting fraternity, the BFSS has made great steps in the shooting world, especially with its education programme, good PR work and excellent shooting video entitled The Shooting Year (*A Three-Legged Stool*).

The BFSS prides itself upon its political clout and, based as it is in London, it is well situated to lobby MPs and committees when the need is there and to react quickly to new developments. In a time of crisis for the shooting world it is unusual to find the BFSS phone unmanned even at weekends and its PR machine is probably one of the best in the sporting world. As with the BASC, membership includes third party insurance for a variety of sporting accidents.

Written and Unwritten

The shooting world is riddled with rules and regulations, some statutory, some not; it is important that they are studied and absorbed if the sportsman is fully to enjoy his sport, keep out of trouble, maintain the reputation of shooting and carry out his responsibilities to the countryside and the quarry. Ignorance of the law is no excuse for trangression. The rough shooter, like any other shooter, must buy a booklet from the BASC with all the rules summarised and make himself an expert in his legal rights and responsibilities.

All country sports and sportsmen are coming under close public scrutiny and the countryside is a far more accessible place than it used to be. Keepers who have employed illegal methods in what they believed to be the most secure and out-of-the-way places have been surprised to find themselves discovered and caught in the act, and dire penalties follow. A protected bird shot by accident in the half-light of a lonely marsh will be witnessed by someone, a bird-watcher, walker, mountain-biker, pony-trekker or one of the growing army of country-users. The shooting man carries on his shoulders the reputation of all others who follow his sport and it behoves him to represent them well and not badly.

The Firearms Amendment Act of 1988 tightened the previously fairly free regime and imposed strict rules on gun owners. A Shotgun Certificate issued by the Chief Constable of the county in which you live is the rule and, with a very few exceptions, you may not hold a shotgun without one. A certificate may be issued to anyone of any age provided the police do not raise an objection, and the burden of proof of unsuitability lies on them. A shotgun certificate is the entitlement of everyone but the applicant may be required to show that he has good reason for wanting to own a gun. Refusal is usually due to a record of criminal behaviour, violence or mental disorder. Invitations to shoot or the chance of a bit of pigeon shooting are quite acceptable as good reasons, and the applicant need not show that he owns land, has a gun in a syndicate or even permission to shoot on a regular basis.

Those under the age of fifteen may not carry or use a gun unless they are accompanied by a certificate holder aged over twenty-one. Those from fifteen to seventeen may use a gun unsupervised but may not buy a gun or ammunition. Those over seventeen must produce a shotgun certificate each time a gun or ammunition is purchased. It is a statutory requirement that the owner keeps all weapons 'in a secure place', which is defined by the Chief Constable and might vary from county to county. In many it has come to mean a steel security cabinet, and many shooting men go to the expense of buying one not for legal reasons but because they treasure their guns and wish to keep their valuable possessions safe from the casual thief.

Keeping weapons out of view of the casual intruder is no more than prudent and some go to the further lengths of removing the fore-end from a shotgun so that it cannot be used in the event of its being stolen.

The semi-automatic and the pump-action shotgun have had their wings clipped by the legislation. The days of loading five cartridges have gone, for the magazine must now be modified to take no more than two with another in the chamber. Both types of weapon have been moved up the scale to Section One firearms (which includes rifles) and they are seen less frequently in the shooting field, due partly to legal restrictions.

It is an offence to shoot on any land where permission has not been granted. Every square inch of ground in the country belongs to someone, be it a county council, the Crown or a local landowner, and the shooting rights will be in hand or disposed of in some other way. The rough shooter who tends to be a wanderer must be well aware of his boundaries, remember that the grass always appears greener on the other side of the fence, and resist temptation. It is Sod's Law that the moment you cross a forbidden boundary you will be seen, and you will lose your shooting and your reputation a good deal more quickly than you acquired them.

Most shooting folk enter into reciprocal agreements with neighbours about gathering shot birds which have fallen over the fence, and it is good advice to get to know the folk next door.

Quarry Lists and Open Seasons

The list of what the British rough shooter can shoot is controlled by a number of different Acts of Parliament. The two most important are the Game Act, 1831 (Game [Scotland] Act, 1832) and the Wildlife and Countryside Act, 1981. The former covers a selection of gamebirds, and the latter covers all other quarry birds. The open seasons are as follows (dates inclusive).

Grouse	12 August–10 December
Ptarmigan (Scotland only)	12 August–10 December
Blackgame	20 August–10 December
Partridge (red-leg and grey)	1 September–1 February
Pheasant	1 October–1 February
Capercaillie	1 October–31 January
Snipe	12 August–31 January
Woodcock (England and Wales)	1 October–31 January
" (Scotland)	1 September–31 January

Coot
Moorhen   } 1 September–31 January
Golden plover

Greylag goose
Pinkfooted goose
Canada goose
Whitefronted goose (England and Wales only)
Mallard
Teal
Pintail   } 1 September–31 January except in or over areas below high water mark of ordinary spring tides, where the season extends to 20 February.
Wigeon
Gadwall
Shoveller
Tufted duck
Pochard
Goldeneye

The Wildlife and Countryside Act 1981 also lists a collection of birds which are considered pest species and which may be shot all the year round. The 'pests list' is as follows.

Wood pigeon	Carrion crow
Collared dove	Hooded crow
Feral pigeon	Magpie
House sparrow	Jay
Starling	Jackdaw
Herring gull	Rook
Lesser black-backed gull	Greater black-backed gull

Rabbits and hares have no close season, except that on moorlands and other un-enclosed non-arable lands, ground game may be shot only by the occupier and persons authorised by him between 11 December (1 July in Scotland) and 31 March.

On a Sunday, shooting gamebirds and hares is against the law in England and Wales; wildfowling is permitted in some counties but not in others. In Scotland it is technically permissible to shoot game on a Sunday but it is customary not to do so and such a practice would be frowned upon, while Sunday wildfowling is illegal. The Sunday shooting of pest species such as pigeons and rabbits is permitted throughout the UK.

My general advice is to avoid shooting on Sunday if at all possible, even in those places where it is legal. Some might argue that this day represents fifty per cent of a rough shooter's time off work, but also on Sunday his activities are conspicuous, and might disturb those who are sensitive about such matters, especially flighting at the crack of dawn when everyone else is trying to enjoy a lie-in. There are six other days a week when with ingenuity he can find a flightline without causing the fuss resulting from Sunday shooting. Like it or not, the modern shooter must be an adept PR man.

Failing total abstinence, use discretion. A flight far from houses in a gale might be acceptable, as would ferreting in remote fields or fowling (in an unrestricted county) miles from anywhere, although even then, the walker and weekender tends to use this day to be out and about. My own rule is not to shoot on Sunday except in very special cases: the reader must make up his own mind about it.

The Game Licence became law under the Act of that name of 1860. It is necessary to have this document if you shoot or attempt to shoot game or take it in any other way, game for the purpose of the Act including pheasant, partridge, grouse, black grouse, ptarmigan, capercaillie, woodcock and snipe. Rabbits and hares are included but most legitimate shooters can find an exemption. No Game Licence is needed for pest species or wildfowl. A Game Licence is available from many Post Offices and costs £6 at the time of writing.

Good manners and sportsmanship apply to the rough shooting field as strictly as to the cricket pitch and the covertside. It does not do to overshoot or be greedy just because, for a series of fluke reasons, you have the quarry at your mercy. Think of another day and of other sportsmen.

Place the sport and enjoyment of others before your own. In company do you take the easy pheasant which blunders into the air in front of you, or do you think of the chap down the line who would, if you left it, have a chance at a hard and faster shot which would give him more pleasure than your shot would give you? If your dog is badly behaved and ranges far off in front of other walking guns, it might very well spoil their sport by flushing game too far off to shoot, in which case you need it on a lead. Use your dog freely to help those without dogs both at hunting and flushing, as well as retrieving their runners. They will do as much for you one day.

It is tempting and often easy to criticise the shooting skills and dog work of others; keep quiet, for who knows when it is your turn to be embarrassed next? Far rather try to help someone who is having trouble; offer to take their unruly dog on a lead until they have sorted themselves out; put them in a likely place if they have had no shots and you have had several; offer to carry the bag of someone who, through age or infirmity, suddenly finds the going a little difficult. Your pace over rough country should be that of the slowest member of the party.

You must become adept at dispatching wounded birds. The haphazard banging and thrashing one sees is unacceptable to a proper sportsman and if he cannot 'pull' the neck of a bird or rabbit, then he must equip himself with a pair of game-dispatching pliers which will do the job quickly and humanely.

All shots should be taken within easy range; long shots are far more unsporting than sitting shots, the latter being justified at non-gamebirds in certain situations such as the result of an arduous stalk. As with Sunday shooting it is up to you, but there is no defence for shooting hopeful long shots in the belief that one day, if you throw enough lead into the sky, something might come down. Many birds and animals will limp away with shot in them as a result of such a foolish, wasteful and cruel practice.

The rough shooter has every right to be following his sport provided he has the proper authorities, permissions and certificates. He has also a grave responsibility which only in recent years has been fully appreciated, to conduct himself in a way which reflects well on himself and his fellows so that his activities are perceived to be a harmonious element of the countryside and not a rapacious intrusion into it.

Epilogue

**There should be no ill-feeling if one gun gets
all the sport**

Rough shooting has remained little changed since those Carolean squires
stalked the coveys of greys over their unkempt acres or crept up on a
paddling of mallard with a spluttering wheel-lock gun. George Morland
painted them and their world in a way which few could equal, but a look at
the sport today shows that the basics remain sacred. It is about hunting,
about finding and outwitting your own quarry and thus about some of the
skills and values which we are in danger of losing in an emasculated age
which regards the countryside through less observant eyes.

The trappings may have changed but such is progress. The beaver hats
and silken hose have been overtaken by more practical wear so that the
modern shooter can enjoy the pleasure of being dry when it rains. Guns
have developed in detail only, and some would say not for the best. I
wonder how it would be were we to return perforce to the days of the
muzzle-loaders? There would be fewer wasted shots, the pace of a shooting
day would become once more leisurely and measured and the risks of
overkill reduced; but perhaps shooting mankind is not yet ready for such a
radical move.

The equipment is new and trendy for those who care about such things,
but a dog, a bag, a gun and a few acres over which to tramp are all that
anyone really needs to take up rough shooting. The grey partridge has all
but gone, but the red-leg partly fills the gap and the pheasant has become
universally common. Wildfowl wax in numbers and grey geese are more
numerous than at any time since the draining of the fens. There is a good list
of shootable species to chase, and while some of the ancient quarry such as

Overleaf:
The fowler homeward plods his weary way

songbirds, which the old-timers shot down with gusto, have very properly been given protection, no one mourns that loss.

The main difference is in the legislation which hems us about, rules created by a new, urbanised society with its inherent fear of guns and lack of understanding of country ways. That great rustic Ralph Whitlock, when asked to defend 'blood sports', replied that they needed no more defence than reaping, ploughing and sowing; in other words, all were seasonal, proper and essential activities, hunting being a small but vital part of the fabric of village life, a countryman's recreation after a year of toil in the fields.

Good luck to all those who march the stubbles, climb the moors, wait by the marshes in early morning and push the rabbits out of the bracken; those who train and work their dogs, carry their bags, make their own gear, brave all weathers and shoot precious little. They come home purged and uplifted men, better prepared than many to face the cruel pressures of life in the 1990s. They have walked in the footprints of their forefathers and the day they may do so no longer will see the British countryside a sadder and diminished place.

EPILOGUE

DAVID & CHARLES' COUNTRY TITLES

BIRDS OF PREY OF THE
BRITISH ISLES
Brian P. Martin

THE COMPLETE GUNDOG
Compiled by John Humphreys

THE COMPLETE ROUGH SHOOT
John Humphreys

CULTIVATING A SHOOT
J.C. Jeremy Hobson

DAYS AND NIGHTS ON
HUNTER'S FEN
John Humphreys

THE FIELDS IN WINTER
Sporting Memories of a Bygone Age
Graham Downing

THE GLORIOUS GROUSE
Brian P. Martin

THE GREAT HUNTS
Foxhunting Countries of the World
Alastair Jackson

THE GREAT SHOOTS
Britain's Premier Sporting Estates
Brian P. Martin

POACHERS' TALES
John Humphreys

JEMIMA PARRY-JONES'
FALCONRY
Care, Captive Breeding and
Conservation
Jemima Parry-Jones

PURDEY'S
The Guns and the Family
Richard Beaumont

SHOOTING PIGEONS
John Humphreys

SPORTING BIRDS OF THE
BRITISH ISLES
Brian P. Martin

THE STORY OF THE SPORTING GUN
Ranulf Rayner

TALES OF THE OLD COUNTRYMEN
Brian P. Martin

TALES OF THE OLD GAMEKEEPERS
Brian P. Martin

WHAT EVERY GUN SHOULD KNOW
J.C. Jeremy Hobson

Index

INDEX